REVISE C3

for MEI Structured Mathematics

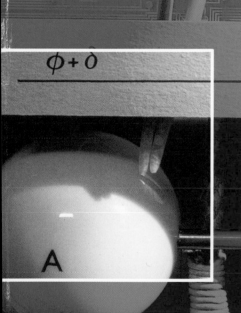

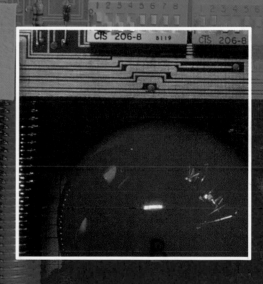

Series Editor
Roger Porkess

Authors
Catherine Berry, Diana Boynova, Sophie Goldie,
Richard Lissaman, Charlie Stripp

HODDER
EDUCATION
AN HACHETTE UK COMPANY

Every effort has been made to trace all copyright holders, but if any have been inadvertently overlooked the Publishers will be pleased to make the necessary arrangements at the first opportunity.

Although every effort has been made to ensure that website addresses are correct at time of going to press, Hodder Education cannot be held responsible for the content of any website mentioned in this book. It is sometimes possible to find a relocated web page by typing in the address of the home page for a website in the URL window of your browser.

Hachette Livre UK's policy is to use papers that are natural, renewable and recyclable products and made from wood grown in sustainable forests. The logging and manufacturing processes are expected to conform to the environmental regulations of the country of origin.

Orders: please contact Bookpoint Ltd, 130 Milton Park, Abingdon, Oxon OX14 4SB.
Telephone: (44) 01235 827720. Fax: (44) 01235 400454. Lines are open 9.00 – 5.00, Monday to Saturday, with a 24-hour message answering service.
Visit our website at www.hoddereducation.co.uk

© Catherine Berry, Diana Boynova, Sophie Goldie, Richard Lissaman,
Roger Porkess, Charlie Stripp, 2009
First published in 2009 by
Hodder Education,
An Hachette UK Company
338 Euston Road
London NW1 3BH

Impression number   5 4 3 2 1
Year   2013 2012 2011 2010 2009

Personal Tutor CD-ROM © Catherine Berry, Diana Boynova, Sophie Goldie, Richard Lissaman, Roger Porkess, Charlie Stripp, 2009; with contributions from Elise Heighway; developed by Infuze Limited; cast: Tom Frankland; recorded at Alchemy Soho.

Typeset in 11/12 Helvetica by Tech-Set Ltd., Gateshead, Tyne & Wear
Printed in Spain

A catalogue record for this title is available from the British Library

ISBN: 978 0 340 957356

Contents

Introduction

Welcome to this Revision Guide for the MEI Core 3 unit!

The book is organised into 14 sections covering the various topics in the syllabus. A typical section is four pages long; the first three pages contain essential information and key worked examples covering the topic.

The last page in each section has questions for you to answer so that you can be sure that you have really understood the topic. There is a multiple-choice exercise and an exam-style question. If you are to gain the greatest possible benefit from the book, and so do your best in the Core 3 exam, you should work through these for yourself and then refer to the accompanying CD to check your answers.

The multiple-choice questions cover the basic ideas and techniques. It is really important that you work through them carefully; guessing will do you no good at all. When you have decided on the answer you think is right, enter it on the CD. If you are right, it tells you so and gives the full solution; check that your answer wasn't just a fluke. If your choice is not right, the CD gives you advice about your mistake; the possible wrong answers have all been designed to pick out particular common misunderstandings. The explanations on the CD are based on the most likely mistakes; even if you make a different mistake, you will usually find enough help to set you on the right path so that you can try again.

When you come on to the exam-style question, write out your best possible answer. Then go to the CD. You will find the solution displayed step-by-step, together with someone talking you through it and giving you helpful advice.

So the book contains the essential information to revise for the exam and, critically, also enables you to check that you have understood it properly. That is a recipe for success.

Finally, a word of warning. This book is designed to be used together with the textbook and not as a replacement for it. This Revision Guide will help you to prepare for the exam but to do really well you also need the deep understanding that comes from the detailed explanations you will find in the textbook.

Good learning and good luck!

Catherine Berry, Diana Boynova, Sophie Goldie, Richard Lissaman,
Roger Porkess, Charlie Stripp

Accompanying books

MEI Structured Mathematics A2 Pure Mathematics C3, C4
ISBN 978 0 340 88851 3

Companion to Advanced Mathematics and Statistics
ISBN 978 0 340 95923 7

Proof

Proof

▶▶ 2

A ABOUT THIS TOPIC

This topic develops the work on constructing a mathematical argument and methods of mathematical proof that were introduced in C1.

R REMEMBER

- The meaning, in a mathematical context, of the terms: 'equals', 'does not equal', 'identically equals', 'therefore', 'because', 'implies', 'is implied by', 'necessary', 'sufficient'.
- The meaning of the following symbols: $=, \neq, \equiv, \therefore, \because, \Rightarrow, \Leftarrow, \Leftrightarrow$
- How to construct and present a mathematical argument.

K KEY FACTS

- A mathematical proof shows whether a mathematical statement (a *conjecture*) is correct in the general case. Once a statement has been proved mathematically, there is no need to check individual examples because the general proof applies to all possible examples.

- There are four types of mathematical proof you must be familiar with:
  1 Proof by direct argument
  2 Proof by exhaustion
  3 Proof by contradiction
  4 Disproof by the use of a counter-example.

Proof by direct argument

This involves expressing the general case of the conjecture (the *conjecture* is the mathematical statement you are trying to prove), and then using the definition of the mathematical property you are testing to see whether it applies to the general case. If it does, the conjecture is true for all cases.

EXAMPLE 1

Prove that the difference between consecutive square numbers is always an odd number.

SOLUTION

To construct this proof you need a general expression for the difference between consecutive square numbers. To test whether a number is odd, you need to use the definition of an odd number, i.e. a number that is not divisible by 2.

If n is a general integer then n^2 and $(n + 1)^2$ are consecutive square numbers.

This means that the difference between consecutive square numbers is of the form $(n + 1)^2 - n^2 = n^2 + 2n + 1 - n^2 = 2n + 1$.

$2n + 1$ is not divisible by 2, so the difference between consecutive square numbers must always be odd.

EXAMPLE 2

Prove that the angle subtended by an arc of a circle at the centre is twice the angle subtended at the circumference by the same arc, i.e. that $y = 2x$ in the diagram. You may assume the result that the angles in a triangle add up to $180°$.

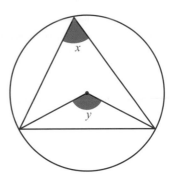

SOLUTION

In the diagram on the right:

The angle subtended by arc AC at the circumference is $\angle ABC$. Call this x.

The angle subtended by arc AC at the centre is $\angle AOC$. Call this y.

Triangles OBC and OBA are isosceles (they each have two sides that are radii of the circle).

So $\angle OBC = \angle OCB = a$ and
$\angle OAB = \angle OBA = b$

So $\angle BOC = 180 - 2a$ and $\angle AOB = 180 - 2b$. ← The angles in a triangle add to 180.
$\Rightarrow 180 - 2a + 180 - 2b = 360 - y$
$\Rightarrow 2a + 2b = y$ ← The angles around the centre point add to 360.
$\Rightarrow y = 2(a + b)$
but $x = a + b$ so $y = 2x$

The angle subtended at the centre is twice the angle subtended at the circumference.

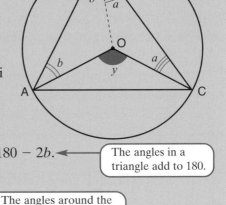

A ADVICE

For proofs of geometric properties it is essential to draw a clear diagram. If often helps to add construction lines, such as line OB in this example, so that you can use known properties of shapes (such as isosceles triangles having two equal angles) to help construct your proof.

Proof by exhaustion

In a proof by exhaustion it is necessary to test every possible case (to exhaust all possibilities).

EXAMPLE 3	Prove that square numbers with two digits are squares of numbers with one digit.

SOLUTION	There are only six square numbers with two digits: 16, 25, 36, 49, 64, 81. The square roots of these numbers are $\pm 4, \pm 5, \pm 6, \pm 7, \pm 8$ and ± 9, all of which are single-digit numbers. Every case has been tested, so the conjecture must be true.

A   ADVICE

Proof by exhaustion is effective when there are only a limited number of cases to check.

Proof by contradiction

In a proof by contradiction you begin by assuming the conjecture you are trying to prove is false and then show that this leads to something that is clearly not true (a contradiction), meaning that the conjecture must actually be true. You can think of this as being a similar argument to an alibi in a criminal case. For example, if you want to prove that a murder suspect, Mrs X, is innocent, you could begin by assuming that she is guilty but then show that because she was in Glasgow at the time when the murder was committed in London, this is a contradiction (Mrs X cannot have been in two places at the same time), so Mrs X must be innocent.

EXAMPLE 4	Prove that $\sqrt{3}$ is irrational.

SOLUTION	Assume that $\sqrt{3}$ is rational, so it can be written in the form $\sqrt{3} = \dfrac{a}{b}$, where a and b are integers with no common factors. $$\sqrt{3} = \frac{a}{b}$$ $$\Rightarrow \quad 3 = \frac{a^2}{b^2}$$ $$\Rightarrow 3b^2 = a^2$$ $\Rightarrow a^2$ is a multiple of 3, so a is a multiple of 3, i.e. $a = 3k$, where k is an integer. $$\Rightarrow 3b^2 = (3k)^2$$ $$\Rightarrow 3b^2 = 9k^2$$ $$\Rightarrow b^2 = 3k^2$$ $\Rightarrow b^2$ is a multiple of 3, so b is a multiple of 3. The proof began by assuming that a and b have no common factors and then showed that, if $\sqrt{3}$ is rational, 3 must be a factor of both a and b. This is a contradiction and therefore $\sqrt{3}$ must be irrational.

Disproof by the use of a counter-example

To prove that a conjecture is false (to disprove it), only one case where it does not work, a counter-example, is required. Counter-examples can be hard to find, but the technique is very powerful because only one is needed to prove a conjecture is false.

EXAMPLE 5   Is it true that $x^2 \geqslant x$ for all real numbers?

SOLUTION   Testing a few numbers, $1^2 = 1$, $50^2 = 2500$, $(-4)^2 = 16$, etc., this looks as if it may be true. However, what about numbers between 0 and 1?

$\left(\dfrac{1}{2}\right)^2 = \dfrac{1}{4}$ and $\dfrac{1}{4} < \dfrac{1}{2}$, showing that it is not true that $x^2 \geqslant x$ for all real numbers.

LINKS

Pure Mathematics   Proof by induction (FP1).
All topics throughout mathematics.

Test Yourself

1   'For all values of n greater than or equal to 1, $n^2 + 3n + 1$ is a prime number.' Which value of n gives a counter-example which disproves this conjecture?

   A $n = 7$ B $n = 2$ C $n = 8$ D $n = 6$

2   Below is a proof that seems to show that $2 = 0$. The proof must contain an error. At which line does the error occur?

$$a = b = 1$$
$$[1] \Rightarrow a^2 = b^2$$
$$[2] \Rightarrow a^2 - b^2 = 0$$
$$[3] \Rightarrow (a + b)(a - b) = 0$$
$$[4] \Rightarrow a + b = 0$$
$$[5] \Rightarrow 2 = 0$$

   A [1]   B [2]   C [4]   D [3]   E [5]

3 Below is an attempt to prove that if an integer, p, is even, p^2 is also even. Is the proof correct, or does it contain an error? If it contains an error, at which line does the error occur?

[1] If p is even then $p = 2k$, where k is an integer.

[2] $\Rightarrow p^2 = (2k)^2 = 4k^2$

[3] $\Rightarrow p^2 = 2(2k^2)$

[4] $\Rightarrow p^2$ is even

A There are no errors in the proof   B [2]   C [3]

D [4]   E [1]

4 Below is an attempt to prove that there is an infinite number of primes.

[1] If there is a finite number of prime numbers, there must be a largest prime number, p_n.

[2] If $p_1, p_2, p_3, \ldots, p_{n-1}$ are all the primes less than p_n then $p_1 \times p_2 \times p_3 \times \ldots \times p_{n-1} \times p_n + 1$ will leave a remainder of 1 when it is divided by any of $p_1, p_2, p_3, \ldots, p_{n-1}, p_n$.

[3] Therefore $p_1 \times p_2 \times p_3 \times \ldots \times p_{n-1} \times p_n + 1$ is prime.

[4] Since $p_1 \times p_2 \times p_3 \times \ldots \times p_{n-1} \times p_n + 1$ must be bigger than p_n, we have a contradiction because we began by stating that p_n was the largest prime.
Therefore there must be an infinite number of prime numbers.

The following five statements refer to this attempted proof. Four of them are false and one of them is true. Which one is true?

A $n = 5$ gives a counter-example because $p_1 \times p_2 \times p_3 \times p_4 \times p_5 + 1 = 121$.

B $n = 3$ gives a counter-example because $p_1 \times p_2 \times p_3 + 1 = 106$ and 106 is not prime.

C $n = 6$ gives a counter-example because $30\,031 = 59 \times 509$.

D $n = 4$ gives a counter-example because $2 \times 3 \times 5 \times 7 + 1 = 211$ and 211 is not prime.

E There are no errors in the proof.

Exam-Style Question

The diagram shows four congruent right-angled triangles with side lengths a, b and c arranged to form a square, with a smaller square 'hole' in the middle.

i) In terms of a and b, what is the area of the square 'hole' in the middle of the diagram?

ii) By expressing the area of the complete diagram in two different ways, prove Pythagoras' theorem.

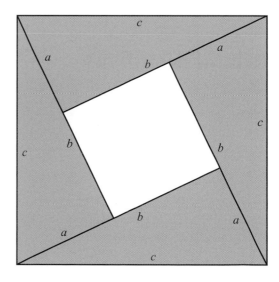

Natural logarithms and exponentials

Natural logarithms

A ABOUT THIS TOPIC

From now on you will only occasionally use logarithms to the base 10. By contrast, you will find that natural logarithms, together with exponential functions, keep cropping up in all sorts of places. So it is really important to understand them well, and not just for the C3 examination.

R REMEMBER

- The laws of indices from GCSE and C1.
- The laws of logarithms from C2.

K KEY FACTS

- $\int \dfrac{1}{x}\,dx = \ln|x| + c$

- $\ln x$ is the natural logarithm of x.
  $\ln x$ can also be written $\log_e x$ where the base e is 2.718….

- If $y = \ln x$, then $x = e^y$.

- e^x is an exponential function.

- e^x and $\ln x$ are inverse functions.

Natural logarithms

Natural logarithms arise because the integral of $\dfrac{1}{x}$ is the natural logarithm of x (or to be more precise, that of the modulus of x, $|x|$). The base of natural logarithms is the number e = 2.718…. The natural logarithm of x is written $\ln x$ or $\log_e x$.

$$\int \frac{1}{x}\,dx = \ln|x| + c$$

Natural logarithms obey the same rules as logs to the base 10, or any other base.

R RULE

$\ln(a \times b) = \ln a + \ln b$ $\ln(a \div b) = \ln a - \ln b$ $\ln\left(\dfrac{1}{a}\right) = -\ln a$

$\ln(a^n) = n \ln a$ $\ln(\sqrt[n]{a}) = \dfrac{1}{n}\ln a$

$\ln 1 = 0$ $\ln e = 1$

Natural logarithms and exponentials

EXAMPLE 1

This is the graph of $y = \dfrac{1}{x}$.

i) Find the area of the shaded region enclosed by the curve, the lines $x = 1$ and $x = 3$ and the x axis.

ii) Find the area of the other shaded region.

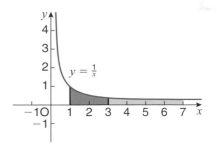

SOLUTION

i) Area $= \displaystyle\int_1^3 \dfrac{1}{x}\, dx = \left[\ln |x|\right]_1^3$

   $= \ln 3 - \ln 1$ ← Remember that $\ln 1 = 0$.

   $= 1.0986... - 0 = 1.099$ units^2 to 3 d.p.

ii) Area $= \displaystyle\int_3^7 \dfrac{1}{x}\, dx = \left[\ln |x|\right]_3^7$

   $= \ln 7 - \ln 3$ ← Remember that $\ln a - \ln b = \ln\left(\dfrac{a}{b}\right)$.

   $= \ln\left(\dfrac{7}{3}\right) = 0.847$ units^2 to 3 d.p.

EXAMPLE 2

The graph shows both branches of $y = \dfrac{2}{x}$. Find the area of the shaded region, formed by the curve, the x axis and the lines $x = -2.5$ and $x = -0.5$.

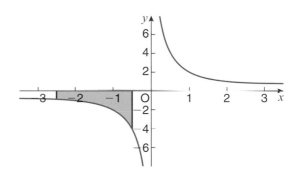

SOLUTION

$\displaystyle\int_{-2.5}^{-0.5} \dfrac{2}{x}\, dx = 2\left[\ln |x|\right]_{-2.5}^{-0.5}$

Notice that $\ln |-0.5| = \ln 0.5$ and $\ln |-2.5| = \ln 2.5$. It is in cases like this, where $x < 0$, that you need the modulus in $\ln |x|$.

   $= 2[\ln (0.5) - \ln (2.5)]$

   $= 2[-0.693... - 0.916...] = -3.2188...$

So the area is 3.219 units^2 to 3 d.p.

Notice that the integral works out to be negative because the region is below the x axis.

The graph of ln x

This is the graph of $y = \ln x$. The negative y axis is an asymptote.

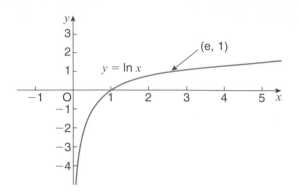

The curve crosses the x axis at (1, 0) and passes through the point (e, 1).

It increases without limit. Notice that for values of x between 0 and 1, ln x is negative.

> ⚠ You can only have the logarithm of a positive number. So if you get, say, ln (-2), something has gone wrong. You have almost certainly made a mistake and should check back.

Exponential functions

If $x = \ln y$, then $y = e^x$. e^x is an exponential function.

Exponential functions obey the usual rules of indices.

$$e^x \times e^y = e^{x+y} \qquad e^x \div e^y = e^{x-y}$$

$$e^1 = e \qquad e^0 = 1 \qquad e^{-1} = \frac{1}{e}$$

Notice that

- e^x is also sometimes written as exp(x).
- The term 'exponential function' is also used for functions such as 2^x and 3^x.
- The exponential and natural logarithm functions are inverses of each other as you can see from their graphs. They are reflections of each other in the line $y = x$.

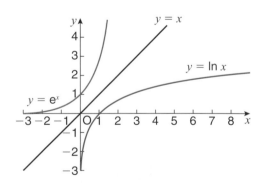

Switching between natural logarithms and exponentials

In each of the next four examples, the first line of the solution sets up relationships like these. With experience you will not need to write these lines down and will start at the second lines.

The key relationships are ln $(e^x) = x$ and $e^{\ln (x)} = x$. Knowing these is the key to success.

EXAMPLE 3

Solve the equation $e^{2x} = 3$.

SOLUTION

Take the ln of both sides: $\ln (e^{2x}) = \ln 3$

$$2x = \ln 3$$

$$x = \frac{\ln 3}{2} = 0.549 \text{ to 3 d.p.}$$

EXAMPLE 4

Make t the subject in $3x + 2 = e^{5t}$.

SOLUTION

Take the ln of both sides: $\ln (3x + 2) = \ln (e^{5t}) = 5t$

$$t = \tfrac{1}{5} \ln (3x + 2)$$

EXAMPLE 5

Make a the subject in $\ln (7a + 1) = 4t$.

SOLUTION

Raise both sides to the power e: $e^{\ln (7a + 2)} = e^{4t}$

$$7a + 2 = e^{4t}$$

$$7a = e^{4t} - 2$$

$$a = \tfrac{1}{7}(e^{4t} - 2)$$

EXAMPLE 6

Make p the subject of $\ln \left(\dfrac{p + 5}{p} \right) = 4t$.

SOLUTION

Raise both sides to the power e: $e^{\left(\frac{p + 5}{p} \right)} = e^{4t}$

$$\frac{p + 5}{p} = e^{4t}$$

$$p + 5 = pe^{4t}$$

$$5 = pe^{4t} - p$$

$$5 = p(e^{4t} - 1)$$

$$p = \frac{5}{e^{4t} - 1}$$

Exponential growth and decay

The graph of $y = e^x$ shows exponential growth. As $x \to \infty$, $y \to \infty$ at an increasing rate.

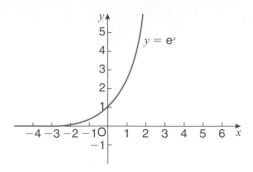

The graph of $y = e^{-x}$ shows exponential decay. As $x \to \infty$, $y \to 0$ at a decreasing rate.

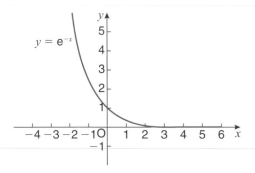

EXAMPLE 7   Sketch the graph of $y = 2 + 3e^{-x}$.

SOLUTION

When $x = 0$,
$y = 2 + 3e^0 = 2 + 3 = 5$.

When $x \to \infty$,
$y \to 2 + 3 \times 0 = 2$.

There is a horizontal asymptote $y = 2$.

A common mistake is to say e^0 is zero whereas in fact $e^0 = 1$.

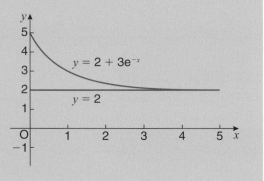

LINKS

Pure Mathematics	Solution of Differential Equations (C4, DE), Curve Sketching (almost everywhere), Hyperbolic Functions (FP2), Complex Numbers (FP2).
Mechanics	Resisted Motion (M4).
Statistics	Poisson Distribution (S2), Exponential Distribution (S3), Generating Functions (S4).

Test Yourself

1 Which of the following is the area of the shaded region?

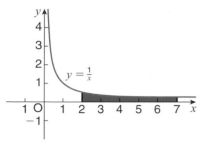

  A $\ln 5$ B $\ln 3.5$ C $\dfrac{1}{4} - \dfrac{1}{49}$ D $\dfrac{\ln 7}{\ln 2}$ E 0.544

2 Make x the subject of the equation $\ln(3x + 2) = 5t$.

  A $x = \frac{1}{3}e^{(5t-2)}$ B $x = \frac{5}{3}(t - \ln 2)$ C $x = \frac{1}{3}(e^{5t} + 2)$ D $x = \frac{1}{3}e^{5t} - 2$ E $x = \frac{1}{3}(e^{5t} - 2)$

3 The graph shows the curve $y = \ln x$.
Four of the following statements are false and
one is true. Which one is true?

  A The graph crosses the y axis at $(0, -1)$.

  B The graph crosses the x axis at $(e, 0)$.

  C The graph passes through the point $(e, 1)$.

  D The graph flattens out for large values of x and
approaches a horizontal asymptote.

  E If you draw the graph for negative values of x,
it is the same curve reflected in the y axis.

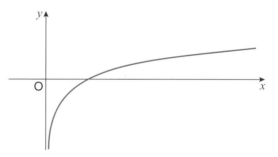

4 You are given that $M = 100 + 300e^{-0.1t}$. Find the value of t when $M = 250$.

  A 4.7 B 50.1 C 0.0693 D 6.93 E -16.5

5 Which of the following is the equation of this curve?

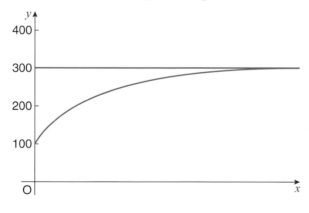

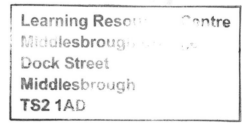

  A $y = 300 - 200e^{-x}$ B $y = 100 + 200e^{-x}$ C $y = 300 - 200e^{x}$

  D $y = 100 + 200e^{x}$ E $y = 200 - 100e^{-x}$

Exam-Style Question

A certain type of parrot is found only in Australia apart from a population which live on a remote island in the south Pacific. It is believed that two of the parrots escaped from a passing ship long ago and established the island's population. The number of parrots on the island, P, has been studied for many years and has been found to be well modelled by the equation

$$P = 5000 - 3000e^{-0.008T}$$

where T is the number of years that have passed since 1900.

i)   Find the number of parrots on the island in (A) 2000 (B) 1900.

ii) In what year will there be 4000 parrots?

iii) Sketch the graph of the number of parrots P against T for $T \geqslant 0$.

iv) Use the equation for P to estimate the year when the two original parrots arrived on the island and give one reason why this might not be very accurate.

v)   Extend your graph to cover values of T less than zero.
     Comment on the main features of the graph.

Exponentials

A | ABOUT THIS TOPIC

Natural logarithms and exponentials are important functions in mathematics and you are expected to become fluent using them in C3. They often arise in long examination questions.

R | REMEMBER

- $\int \dfrac{1}{x}\,dx = \ln|x| + c$ from C3.
- If $y = e^x$, then $\ln y = x$ from C3.
- Natural logarithms and exponentials are inverse functions.

K | KEY FACTS

- If $y = \ln x$, $\dfrac{dy}{dx} = \dfrac{1}{x}$.
- To find $\int \ln x\,dx$, use integration by parts from C3.
- If $y = e^{ax}$, $\dfrac{dy}{dx} = ae^{ax}$.
- $\int e^{ax}\,dx = \dfrac{1}{a}e^{ax} + c$.

Using calculus with natural logarithms

You know from the last section that $\int \dfrac{1}{x}\,dx = \ln|x| + c$, so it follows that the derivative of $\ln x$ is $\dfrac{1}{x}$. If $y = \ln x$, then $\dfrac{dy}{dx} = \dfrac{1}{x}$.

The next two examples show you how to differentiate some related functions.

EXAMPLE 1

Differentiate $y = \ln 5x$.

SOLUTION

$$y = \ln 5x$$
$$= \ln 5 + \ln x$$

> Using the rule $\ln(ab) = \ln a + \ln b$.

$$\Rightarrow \frac{dy}{dx} = 0 + \frac{1}{x} = \frac{1}{x}$$

> $\ln 5$ is a constant so differentiating it gives zero.

EXAMPLE 2

Differentiate $y = \ln x^7$.

SOLUTION

$$y = \ln x^7$$
$$= 7\ln x$$

> Using the rule $\ln(x^n) = n\log x$.

$$\Rightarrow \frac{dy}{dx} = 7 \times \frac{1}{x} = \frac{7}{x}$$

The usual method of integrating $\ln x$ is to use integration by parts which is covered in Chapter 5.

It tells you that $\int \ln x \, dx = x \ln x - x + c$.

 You are better not to try to remember the result for $\int \ln x \, dx$. Instead make sure that you can work it out for yourself. When you are revising integration by parts, remember that you may have to do it in the examination.

Using calculus with exponentials

Remember that if $y = e^{ax}$, then $\dfrac{dy}{dx} = ae^{ax}$.

The equivalent result for integrating e^{ax} is

$$\int e^{ax} \, dx = \frac{1}{a} e^{ax} + c$$

A particularly easy case is when $a = 1$.

$$y = e^x \Rightarrow \frac{dy}{dx} = e^x$$

EXAMPLE 3   Given that $y = e^x - 2e^{-3x}$, find $\dfrac{dy}{dx}$.

SOLUTION

$$y = e^x - 2e^{-3x}$$

$$\Rightarrow \frac{dy}{dx} = e^x - 2 \times (-3)e^{-3x}$$

$$= e^x + 6e^{-3x}$$

EXAMPLE 4   The shaded region in the diagram is bounded by the curve $y = \frac{1}{2}e^{3x}$, the lines $x = 0.4$ and $x = 0.8$ and the x axis. Find its area to 2 decimal places.

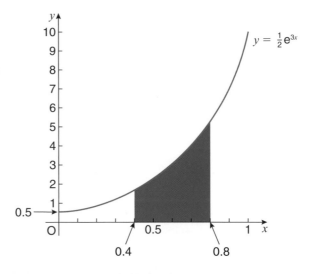

SOLUTION   The area is $\displaystyle\int_{0.4}^{0.8} \frac{1}{2} e^{3x} \, dx$

$$= \left[\frac{1}{2} \times \frac{1}{3} e^{3x} \right]_{0.4}^{0.8}$$

$$= \frac{1}{6} e^{2.4} - \frac{1}{6} e^{1.2}$$

$$= 1.2838\ldots$$

$$= 1.28 \text{ to } 2 \text{ d.p.}$$

Questions are often set about the graphs of functions involving natural logarithms and exponentials, like that in the next example and also in the exam-style question.

Natural logarithms and exponentials

2

EXAMPLE 5

The function $f(x) = e^x - \ln x$ for $x > 0$.

i) Explain the restriction $x > 0$.

ii) Show that $f(x)$ has a minimum value between $x = 0.5$ and $x = 0.6$.

iii) Sketch the curve $y = f(x)$ for $0 < x \leqslant 1$.

SOLUTION

i) The function $f(x)$ includes $\ln x$, which is only defined for positive values of x, so $f(x)$ is only defined for $x > 0$.

ii) $f(x) = e^x - \ln x$

$$\Rightarrow f'(x) = e^x - \frac{1}{x}$$

For a stationary point $f'(x) = 0$

and so $\qquad\qquad e^x - \dfrac{1}{x} = 0$

The equation cannot be solved analytically, it can only be solved numerically. Since

$$f'(0.5) = e^{0.5} - \frac{1}{0.5} = -0.351\ldots \quad \text{and} \quad f'(0.6) = e^{0.6} - \frac{1}{0.6} = 0.155,$$

there is a value of x between 0.5 and 0.6 for which $f(x) = 0$.

The gradient goes from negative through zero to positive so this stationary point is a minimum.

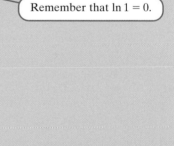

iii) The negative y axis is an asymptote for $\ln x$ so the positive y axis is an asymptote for $-\ln x$ and so for $f(x)$.

When $x = 1$, $f(x) = e^1 + \ln 1 = e + 0 = e$

So the graph looks like this.

Remember that $\ln 1 = 0$.

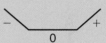

LINKS

Pure Mathematics	Solution of Differential Equations (C4, DE), Curve Sketching (almost everywhere), Hyperbolic Functions (FP2), Complex Numbers (FP2).
Mechanics	Resisted Motion (M4).
Statistics	Poisson Distribution (S2), Exponential Distribution (S3), Generating Functions (S4).

Test Yourself

1   Differentiate $y = \ln 2x$.

   A $\dfrac{dy}{dx} = \ln 2 + \dfrac{1}{x}$ B $\dfrac{dy}{dx} = \dfrac{2}{x}$ C $\dfrac{dy}{dx} = \dfrac{1}{2x}$ D $\dfrac{dy}{dx} = \dfrac{1}{x}$

2   Differentiate $y = 3 \ln \left(\dfrac{1}{x^5} \right)$.

   A $\dfrac{dy}{dx} = -\dfrac{15}{x}$ B $\dfrac{dy}{dx} = -\dfrac{5}{x}$ C $\dfrac{dy}{dx} = \dfrac{15}{x}$ D $\dfrac{dy}{dx} = -15 \ln \left(\dfrac{1}{x^6} \right)$

3   Given that $y = 6e^{4x}$, find $\dfrac{dy}{dx}$.

   A $4e^{4x}$ B $\dfrac{3}{2}e^{4x}$ C $24e^{4x}$ D $24e^{4x-1}$

4   The shaded region in this graph is formed by the curves
$y = e^{3x}$, $y = e^{2x}$ and $x = 2$.
Find the area of the region.

   A $\dfrac{1}{3}e^6 - \dfrac{1}{2}e^4 + \dfrac{1}{6}$ B $\dfrac{1}{3}e^6 - \dfrac{1}{2}e^4$

   C $e^2 - 1$ D $3e^6 - 2e^4 - 1$

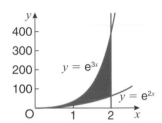

Exam-Style Question

The graph shows the curve $y = e^x$ and the line $y = p$. It is drawn with equal
scales along the x axis and y axis. The line $y = p$ cuts the curve at the point
P. The region between the curve, the y axis and the line $y = p$ is shaded.

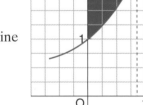

i)   Find the co-ordinates of P.

ii)   Find the area of the region bounded by the curve, the axes and the line
    through P parallel to the y axis.
    Hence find the area of the shaded region.

iii)   Copy the graph and then draw on it a sketch of $y = \ln x$.
     Shade the region bounded by the curve $y = \ln x$, the
     x axis and the line $x = p$.

iv)   Write down, in terms of p, the value of $\displaystyle\int_1^p \ln x \, dx$.

Functions

The language of functions

19 25, 36 39, 56

A | ABOUT THIS TOPIC

A mapping is any rule which associates two sets of items. In mathematics, a mapping often transforms one set of numbers into another set of numbers. In this section you look at some of the terminology associated with mappings and functions.

R | REMEMBER

- Shapes of basic graphs such as polynomial graphs and trigonometric graphs from C1 and C2.
- $x \in \mathbb{R}$ means that x is a member of the set of real numbers.

K | KEY FACTS

- A **mapping** transforms each **object** from the **domain** to an **image** or images in the **co-domain**. The **range** is the set of image points within the co-domain.

- A **function** is a mapping which is **one-to-one** or **many-to-one**.

- A mapping which is **one-to-many** or **many-to-many** is not a function.

- A function f is **odd** if $f(-x) = -f(x)$. The graph of an odd function has rotational symmetry about the origin.

- A function f is **even** if $f(-x) = f(x)$. The graph of an even function is symmetrical about the y axis.

- A **periodic** function is a function whose graph has a repeating pattern.

The language of mappings

A mapping is a rule which links items in one set to items in another set.

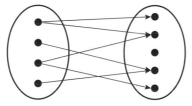

This set is called the **domain**.

The items in the domain are called **objects**.

This set is called the **co-domain**.

The items in the co-domain are called **images**.

The set of image points is called the **range**. Often, the range is the same set as the co-domain. However, in the example above there is a point in the co-domain which is not in the range, so the two sets are different.

The mapping shown above is a **many-to-many** mapping. Some points in the domain map to more than one image, and some points in the co-domain are the image of more than one point in the domain.

In a **many-to-one** mapping, each point in the domain maps to just one image point, but some points in the co-domain are the image of more than one point in the domain.

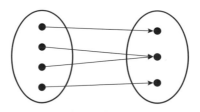

In a **one-to-many** mapping, some points in the domain map to more than one image, but each point in the co-domain is the image of just one object point.

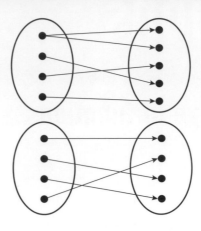

In a **one-to-one** mapping, each point in the domain maps to just one image point, and each point in the co-domain is the image of just one object point.

Functions

A function is a mapping in which each point in the domain maps to just one image point. So a function is a many-to-one or a one-to-one mapping.

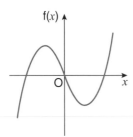

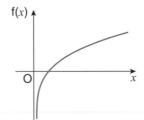

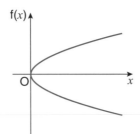

This is a many-to-one function, with domain $x \in \mathbb{R}$ and range $f(x) \in \mathbb{R}$.

This is a one-to-one function, with domain $x > 0$ and range $f(x) \in \mathbb{R}$.

This is **not** a function. It is a one-to-many mapping, with domain $x > 0$ and range $f(x) \in \mathbb{R}$.

EXAMPLE 1

The function f is defined by $f(x) = (x - 2)^2 - 1$ for $x \in \mathbb{R}$.

i) Sketch the graph of $y = f(x)$ and write down the range of f.
ii) Find $f(-3)$.
iii) Find the values of x for which $f(x) = 3$.

SOLUTION

i) This is a quadratic function, with minimum point $(2, -1)$.

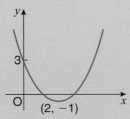

The range of f is $f(x) \geqslant -1$.

ii) $f(-3) = (-3 - 2)^2 - 1 = (-5)^2 - 1 = 25 - 1 = 24$

iii) $f(x) = 3 \Rightarrow (x - 2)^2 - 1 = 3$
$$\Rightarrow (x - 2)^2 = 4$$
$$\Rightarrow x - 2 = \pm\sqrt{4}$$
$$\Rightarrow x = 2 \pm 2 = 0 \text{ or } 4$$

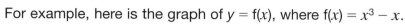
Odd and even functions

A function is **odd** if $f(-x) = -f(x)$.

The graph of an odd function has rotational symmetry of order 2 about the origin.

For example, here is the graph of $y = f(x)$, where $f(x) = x^3 - x$.

$f(-x) = (-x)^3 - (-x) = -x^3 + x = -(x^3 - x) = -f(x)$

so this function is odd.

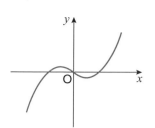

A function is **even** if $f(-x) = f(x)$.

The graph of an even function is symmetrical about the y axis.

For example, here is the graph of $y = g(x)$, where $g(x) = \dfrac{x^2 + 1}{x^2 - 1}$.

$g(-x) = \dfrac{(-x)^2 + 1}{(-x)^2 - 1} = \dfrac{x^2 + 1}{x^2 - 1} = g(x)$

so this function is even.

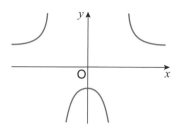

 Not all functions are odd or even. Many are neither!

Periodic functions

A **periodic** function is a function which has a repeating pattern. The **period** of the function is the difference between the values of x at the start and end of one repeated pattern within the function. So for a function with period k, $f(x + k) = f(x)$ for all values of x.

The trigonometric functions $\sin x$, $\cos x$ and $\tan x$ are all periodic functions. The functions $\sin x$ and $\cos x$ both have periods of 2π, and $\tan x$ has a period of π.

EXAMPLE 2 A function g has period 2 and is defined by

$$g(x) = 1 - x^2 \quad \text{for} \quad -1 \leqslant x \leqslant 1.$$

i) Sketch the graph of $y = g(x)$ for $-5 \leqslant x \leqslant 5$.
ii) State the range of the function g.

SOLUTION **i)**

Sketch the graph of $y = 1 - x^2$ for $-1 \leqslant x \leqslant 1$.

Repeat the pattern elsewhere.

ii) The range of g is $0 \leqslant g(x) \leqslant 1$.

LINKS

Pure Mathematics Functions are used throughout Pure Mathematics.
Statistics Functions are used in S1 and S3 to define Random Variables.

Test Yourself

1 The mapping $x \to \sqrt[3]{x^2 - 1}$, $x \in \mathbb{R}$, can be described as

    A one-to-one   B one-to-many   C many-to-one   D many-to-many

2 The function f is defined as f: $x \to \sqrt{2x - 3}$.
What is the domain of f?

    A $x \in \mathbb{R}$ B $x \geqslant 0$ C $x \geqslant \frac{3}{2}$ D $x \geqslant 3$

3 The function g is defined as $g(x) = x^2 - 2x - 1$ for $-2 \leqslant x \leqslant 2$.
What is the range of the function?

    A $-1 \leqslant g(x) \leqslant 7$ B $g(x) \leqslant 7$ C $g(x) \geqslant -2$ D $-2 \leqslant g(x) \leqslant 7$

4 The function f is defined as $f(x) = x^3 \cos x$.

The function g is defined as $g(x) = \dfrac{(x - 1)^2}{x^2 + 1}$.

Which one of these statements is true?

    A f is an odd function; g is an even function.

    B f is an odd function; g is neither odd nor even.

    C f is neither odd nor even; g is an odd function.

    D f is an even function; g is neither odd nor even.

    E f is an even function; g is an odd function.

5 What is the period of the function $f(x) = \tan 3x$?

    A $\frac{1}{3}$ B 3π C 3   D $\frac{2}{3}\pi$ E $\frac{1}{3}\pi$

Exam-Style Question

The function $f(x)$ is defined by $f(x) = \dfrac{x^3}{(x + 3)(x - 3)}$ for $-2 \leqslant x \leqslant 2$.

The diagram shows a sketch of the graph of $y = f(x)$.

i) Find the range of the function $f(x)$.

ii) Show algebraically that $f(x)$ is an odd function.
State how this property relates to the shape of the curve.

The function $g(x)$ is defined by $g(x) = \dfrac{x^2}{(x + 3)(x - 3)}$ for $-2 \leqslant x \leqslant 2$.

iii) Use algebra to determine whether $g(x)$ is odd, even or neither odd nor even.

iv) Find $g(0)$, $g(1)$ and $g(2)$ and hence sketch the graph of $y = g(x)$ for $-2 \leqslant x \leqslant 2$.

Composite functions and transformations

A ABOUT THIS TOPIC

This topic looks at composite functions, in which you apply a function, and then apply a second function to the result. This idea is important in C3 Chain rule, on differentiation using the chain rule, and in C3 Integration by substitution.

A particular application of this work is in combined transformations of graphs. This topic extends the work you did on translations and stretches of graphs in C1 and C2, to include reflections of graphs, and combinations of two or more of these transformations.

R REMEMBER

- Translations of graphs from C1, and stretches of graphs from C2.
- Shapes of basic graphs such as polynomial graphs and trigonometric graphs from C1 and C2.

K KEY FACTS

- The composite function $gf(x)$ is the result of first applying function f to x, to get $f(x)$, then applying function g to the result, to get $g[f(x)]$ or $gf(x)$.

- The following graphs can be obtained by transformations of the graph of $y = f(x)$.

$f(x - a) + b$	Translation through $\begin{pmatrix} a \\ b \end{pmatrix}$
$af(x)$	Stretch parallel to the y axis, scale factor a
$f(ax)$	Stretch parallel to the x axis, scale factor $\dfrac{1}{a}$
$f(-x)$	Reflection in the y axis
$-f(x)$	Reflection in the x axis

Composite functions

If you apply a function f to x to give $f(x)$, and then apply another function g to the result, giving $g[f(x)]$ or $gf(x)$, then you have applied the composite function gf to x.

EXAMPLE 1	The functions f and g are defined as follows:

$$f(x) = 2x - 1 \qquad x \in \mathbb{R}$$
$$g(x) = \sqrt{x} \qquad x \geqslant 0$$

Find

i) $fg(x)$

ii) $gf(x)$

> Remember $\sqrt{x}$ means the positive square root of x.

giving the domain and range of the composite function in each case.

SOLUTION

i) $g(x) = \sqrt{x}$

$fg(x) = f(\sqrt{x})$ ← [Apply the function f to $\sqrt{x}$.]

$= 2\sqrt{x} - 1$

The domain is $x \geqslant 0$ since $\sqrt{x}$ does not exist for $x < 0$.

The smallest possible value of $\sqrt{x}$ is 0, so $2\sqrt{x} - 1 \geqslant -1$. So the range is $fg(x) \geqslant -1$.

ii) $f(x) = 2x - 1$

$gf(x) = g(2x - 1)$ ← [Apply the function g to $2x - 1$.]

$= \sqrt{2x - 1}$

Since $\sqrt{2x - 1}$ does not exist for $2x - 1 < 0$, the domain is $x \geqslant \frac{1}{2}$.

The smallest possible value of $\sqrt{2x - 1}$ is 0, and so the range is $gf(x) \geqslant 0$.

Example 1 illustrates some important points.

- $fg(x)$ is not the same as $gf(x)$. This is the case for most composite functions, although not in every case.
- You need to be careful with domains and ranges for composite functions. The domain for a composite function may not be the same as the domain for either of the functions involved.

Transformations of graphs

You will need to know the following transformations:

Translations

- The graph of $y = f(x - a)$ is obtained from the graph of $y = f(x)$ by a translation of a units in the positive x direction.
- The graph of $y = f(x) + a$ is obtained from the graph of $y = f(x)$ by a translation of a units in the positive y direction.

Stretches

- The graph of $y = af(x)$ is obtained from the graph of $y = f(x)$ by a stretch, scale factor a, parallel to the y axis.
- The graph of $y = f(ax)$ is obtained from the graph of $y = f(x)$ by a stretch, scale factor $\frac{1}{a}$, parallel to the x axis.

Reflections

- The graph of $y = -f(x)$ is obtained from the graph of $y = f(x)$ by a reflection in the x axis.
- The graph of $y = f(-x)$ is obtained from the graph of $y = f(x)$ by a reflection in the y axis.

Reflections are really just a special case of stretches, with scale factor -1.

Combining transformations

You need to be able to work with combinations of two or more transformations. A combination of transformations works in the same way as a composite function: you apply the second transformation to the result of the first. As with composite functions, the result can be different if you carry out the transformations in a different order.

EXAMPLE 2

Find the equation of the new graph when the following transformations are applied to the graph of $y = \sin x$.

i) A stretch, scale factor 2, parallel to the y axis, followed by a translation of 1 unit vertically downwards.

ii) A translation of 1 unit vertically downwards, followed by a stretch, scale factor 2, parallel to the y axis.

Sketch the new graph in each case.

SOLUTION

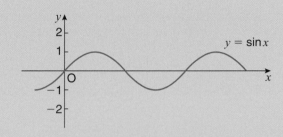

i) A stretch, scale factor 2, parallel to the y axis, maps the graph of $y = \sin x$ to the graph of $y = 2 \sin x$.
A translation of 1 unit vertically downwards maps the graph of $y = 2 \sin x$ to the graph of $y = 2 \sin x - 1$.

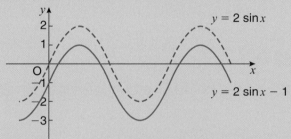

ii) A translation of 1 unit vertically downwards maps the graph of $y = \sin x$ to the graph of $y = \sin x - 1$.
A stretch, scale factor 2, parallel to the y axis, maps the graph of $y = \sin x - 1$ to the graph of $y = 2(\sin x - 1)$, or $y = 2 \sin x - 2$.

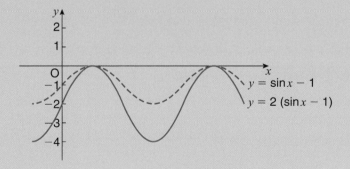

EXAMPLE 3

Show how the graph of $y = -(x + 1)^3$ can be obtained from the graph of $y = x^3$ using successive transformations, and hence sketch the graph of $y = -(x + 1)^3$.

The graph of $y = x^3$ can be mapped to the graph of $y = (x + 1)^3$ by a translation of 1 unit to the left.

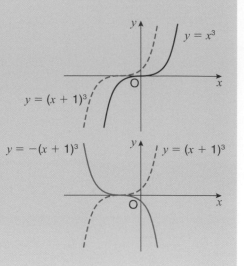

The graph of $y = (x + 1)^3$ can be mapped to the graph of $y = -(x + 1)^3$ by a reflection in the x axis.

LINKS

Pure Mathematics   Transformations are used in all graph work throughout Pure Mathematics. The idea of composite functions is needed for the work in C3 Chain rule on differentiation using the chain rule and in C3 Integration by substitution. It is also used in the work on Matrix Transformations in FP1.

Test Yourself

1 The functions f and g are defined for all real numbers x as

$$f(x) = x^2 - 2, \qquad g(x) = 3 - 2x$$

Find an expression for the function $fg(x)$ (for all real numbers x).

A $fg(x) = 7 - 2x^2$

B $fg(x) = -2x^3 + 3x^2 + 4x - 6$

C $fg(x) = 4x^2 - 12x + 7$

D $fg(x) = 7 + 4x^2$

E $fg(x) = 1 - 2x^2$

2 The functions p and q are defined as follows:

$$p(x) = \frac{1}{x} \quad x \neq 0, \quad q(x) = 2x - 1 \quad x \in \mathbb{R}$$

Find an expression for the function pq.

A $pq(x) = \dfrac{2}{x} - 1, \qquad x \neq 0$

B $pq(x) = \dfrac{2}{x} - 1, \qquad x \in \mathbb{R}$

C $pq(x) = \dfrac{1}{2x - 1}, \qquad x \neq 0$

D $pq(x) = \dfrac{1}{2x - 1}, \qquad x \in \mathbb{R}$

E $pq(x) = \dfrac{1}{2x - 1}, \qquad x \neq \dfrac{1}{2}$

3 The graph of $y = x^2$ is first translated 2 units to the right and 1 unit vertically upwards, and then reflected in the y axis.
Which of the following is the equation of the new graph?

A $y = x^2 + 4x + 5$ B $y = -x^2 + 4x - 5$ C $y = x^2 - 4x + 5$ D $y = -x^2 - 4x - 5$

4 The graph of $y = f(x)$ has a maximum point at $(-3, 2)$.
Which of the following is the maximum point of the graph of $y = 2 + 3f(x)$?

A $(-3, 12)$ B $(-7, 8)$ C $(-1, 4)$ D $(-3, 8)$

Exam-Style Question

The functions f(x) and g(x) are defined for all real numbers x by

$$f(x) = \cos x, \qquad g(x) = 1 - x$$

where x is measured in radians.

i) Find the composite functions fg(x) and gf(x).

ii) State a sequence of two transformations that would map the curve $y = f(x)$ on to the curve $y = gf(x)$.
Sketch the curves $y = f(x)$ and $y = gf(x)$ on the same axes, for $-2\pi \leqslant x \leqslant 2\pi$, indicating clearly which is which.

Inverse functions

A ABOUT THIS TOPIC

In this topic you look at inverse functions, which 'undo' the effect of a function. Some important examples of inverse functions are the inverse trigonometric functions.

R REMEMBER

- Functions from C3.
- Rearranging a formula from C1.
- The graphs of the trigonometric functions from C2.

K KEY FACTS

- Any one-to-one function $f(x)$ has an inverse function $f^{-1}(x)$ which reverses the effect of the function.
- The graphs of a function and its inverse function are reflections of each other in the line $y = x$.
- The arcsine, arccosine and arctangent functions are the inverse functions of the sine, cosine and tangent functions, with their domains restricted so that they are one-to-one functions.

Inverse functions

The inverse of a function 'undoes' the effect of a function.

The inverse of a function $f(x)$ is written as $f^{-1}(x)$.

For example, the inverse of the function $f(x) = x + 2$ is $f^{-1}(x) = x - 2$, because subtracting 2 undoes the effect of adding 2.

For a function f to have an inverse function f^{-1}, then f must be a one-to-one function over the domain of f. The range of f is the same as the domain of f^{-1}, and the domain of f is the same as the range of f^{-1}.

Finding the inverse of a function

To find the inverse of a function:
- Write the function in the form $y = f(x)$.
- Interchange y and x, to give $x = f(y)$.
- Rearrange to make y the subject.

EXAMPLE 1

The function f is defined as $f(x) = 3x^2 - 2 \qquad x \geq 0$.
Find the inverse of f.

SOLUTION

Write the function in the form $y = f(x)$: $\qquad y = 3x^2 - 2$

Interchange y and x, to give $x = f(y)$: $\qquad x = 3y^2 - 2$

Rearrange to make y the subject: $\qquad x + 2 = 3y^2$ ← Add 2 to each side.

Divide each side by 3. → $\dfrac{x + 2}{3} = y^2$

Take the square root of each side. → $\sqrt{\dfrac{x + 2}{3}} = y$

The range of the function f is $f(x) \geq -2$, so the domain of f^{-1} is $x \geq -2$.

The inverse of f is $f^{-1}(x) = \sqrt{\dfrac{x + 2}{3}} \qquad x \geq -2$.

Inverse functions and their graphs

The graphs of a function and its inverse are reflections of each other in the line $y = x$.

For example, the diagram shows graphs of the functions f and f^{-1} from example 1.

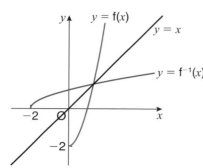

> Remember that for the line $y = x$ to be at 45° to the axes, the x and y scales must be the same.

EXAMPLE 2

The function g is defined as $g(x) = 1 + e^x$.

i) Find an expression for $g^{-1}(x)$, stating the domain of this function.
ii) Sketch the graphs of $y = g(x)$ and $y = g^{-1}(x)$ on the same axes.

SOLUTION

i) Write the function in the form $y = g(x)$: $\qquad y = 1 + e^x$

Interchange y and x, to give $x = g(y)$: $\qquad x = 1 + e^y$

Rearrange to make y the subject: $\qquad x - 1 = e^y$

$$\ln(x - 1) = y$$

The range of the function g is $g(x) > 1$ so the domain of g^{-1} is $x > 1$.

The inverse of g is $g^{-1}(x) = \ln(x - 1)$, $x > 1$.

> Remember that $e^x > 0$ for all x. Since $g(x) = 1 + e^x$, $g(x) > 1$.

ii)

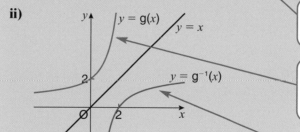

> The graph of $y = 1 + e^x$ is obtained by translating the graph of $y = e^x$ by 1 unit vertically upwards.

> The graph of $y = g^{-1}(x)$ is the reflection of the graph of $y = g(x)$ in the line $y = x$.

The inverse trigonometric functions

The trigonometric functions sin, cos and tan are not one-to-one functions, so they do not have inverse functions. However, if the domain of the trigonometric functions is restricted so that they are one-to-one over this restricted domain, they do have inverse functions, which are called arcsin, arccos and arctan. In some textbooks these inverse trigonometric functions are written as $\sin^{-1}$, $\cos^{-1}$ and $\tan^{-1}$.

For the sine function, the domain is restricted to $-\frac{1}{2}\pi \leq x \leq \frac{1}{2}\pi$.

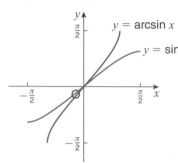

For the cosine function, the domain is restricted to $0 \leq x \leq \pi$.

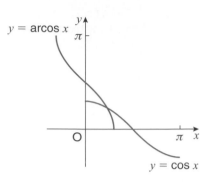

For the tangent function, the domain is restricted to $-\frac{1}{2}\pi < x < \frac{1}{2}\pi$.

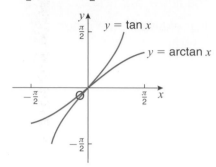

EXAMPLE 3

The function f(x) is defined by $f(x) = 1 + 2\sin x$ for $-\frac{1}{2}\pi \leq x \leq \frac{1}{2}\pi$.

Find an expression for $f^{-1}(x)$, and state the domain of this function.

SOLUTION

$$y = 1 + 2\sin x$$

Interchanging x and y: $\quad x = 1 + 2\sin y$

$$x - 1 = 2\sin y$$

$$\frac{x-1}{2} = \sin y$$

$$\arcsin\left(\frac{x-1}{2}\right) = y$$

> $-1 \leq \sin y \leq 1$, so
> $-2 \leq 2\sin y \leq 2$, so
> $-1 \leq 1 + 2\sin y \leq 3$.

The range of the function f is $-1 \leq f(x) \leq 3$, so the domain of f^{-1} is

$-1 \leq x \leq 3$. $f^{-1}(x) = \arcsin\left(\frac{x-1}{2}\right)$ for $-1 \leq x \leq 3$.

LINKS

Pure Mathematics
The idea of inverse functions is also used in the work on Matrix Transformations in FP1.

Test Yourself

1 The function f is defined by $f(x) = 2x^3 - 1$.
   Find the inverse function f^{-1}.

   A $f^{-1}(x) = \dfrac{\sqrt[3]{x+1}}{2}$

   B $f^{-1}(x) = \dfrac{1}{2x^3 - 1}$

   C $f^{-1}(x) = \sqrt[3]{\dfrac{x+1}{2}}$

   D $f^{-1}(x) = \dfrac{\sqrt[3]{x}+1}{2}$

2 The diagram shows the graph of $y = g(x)$.

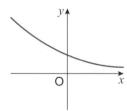

   Which of the diagrams below shows the graph of $y = g^{-1}(x)$?

   A 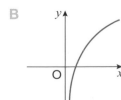 B C 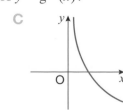 D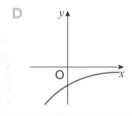

3 The function f is defined by $f(x) = \ln(2x - 1)$ $x > \frac{1}{2}$.
The inverse function f^{-1} is defined by

A $f^{-1}(x) = e^{2x-1}$ $x > \frac{1}{2}$ B $f^{-1}(x) = e^{2x-1}$ $x \in \mathbb{R}$

C $f^{-1}(x) = \frac{1}{2}(e^x + 1)$ $x > \frac{1}{2}$ D $f^{-1}(x) = \frac{1}{2}(e^x + 1)$ $x \in \mathbb{R}$

4 The function $f(x)$ is defined by $f(x) = 1 + \sin 2x$. The domain of x is restricted so that the function has an inverse, $f^{-1}(x)$. Three of the following statements are false and one is true. Which one is true?

A $f^{-1}(x) = \arcsin\left(\dfrac{x-1}{2}\right)$

B   The domain of x could be $-2\pi \leqslant x \leqslant 2\pi$

C   The domain of $f^{-1}(x)$ is $-1 \leqslant x \leqslant 3$

D   If the range of $f(x)$ is $a \leqslant x \leqslant b$, then $b - a \leqslant 2$

5 The function g is defined by $g(x) = 2\tan\left(x - \dfrac{\pi}{2}\right)$ $0 < x < \pi$.

The inverse function g^{-1} is defined by

A $g^{-1}(x) = \arctan\left(\dfrac{1}{2}x\right) + \dfrac{\pi}{2}$ $x \in \mathbb{R}$ B $g^{-1}(x) = \arctan\left(\dfrac{1}{2}x\right) + \dfrac{\pi}{2}$ $0 < x < \pi$

C $g^{-1}(x) = \dfrac{\pi}{2} + \dfrac{1}{2}\arctan x$ $x \in \mathbb{R}$ D $g^{-1}(x) = \dfrac{\pi}{2} + \dfrac{1}{2}\arctan x$ $0 < x < \pi$

Exam-Style Question

The function f is defined by $f(x) = 1 + \cos 2x$ for $0 \leqslant x \leqslant \frac{1}{2}\pi$.

i)   Sketch the graph of $y = f(x)$.

ii)   Find an expression for $f^{-1}(x)$, and state its domain and range.

iii)   Add a sketch of $y = f^{-1}(x)$ to your sketch from i).

The modulus function

A | ABOUT THIS TOPIC

This section is about the modulus function. The modulus of a number is its positive numerical value, so the modulus function is positive everywhere. You can use graphs of modulus functions to help you to solve equations and inequalities.

R | REMEMBER

- Graphs of simple functions from C1.
- Solution of inequalities from C1.

K | KEY FACTS

- The modulus of x, written $|x|$, means the positive value of x.

The modulus function

The modulus of x means the positive (or absolute) value of x, and is written as $|x|$.

So the equation $|x| = 2$ has two roots: $x = 2$ and $x = -2$.

This is the graph of the modulus function. Notice that the graph has two branches. The branch on the right, for $x > 0$, is part of the line $y = x$, and the branch on the left, for $x < 0$, is part of the line $y = -x$.

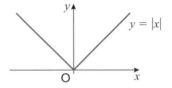

You can use transformations to sketch other graphs involving a modulus sign.

EXAMPLE 1

Sketch the graph of $y = 1 - |x|$.

SOLUTION

Start with the graph $y = |x|$.	The graph $y = -|x|$ is obtained from the graph of $y = |x|$ by a reflection in the x axis.	The graph $y = 1 - |x|$ is obtained from the graph of $y = -|x|$ by a translation of 1 unit vertically upwards.
		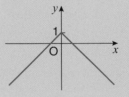

To sketch the graph of the function $y = |f(x)|$, start by sketching the graph of $y = f(x)$, and then reflect the negative part of the graph in the x axis, as in the next example.

EXAMPLE 2

Sketch the graph of $y = |x - 2|$.

SOLUTION

Start by sketching the graph of $y = x - 2$. This graph passes through the points $(0, -2)$ and $(2, 0)$.

Now reflect the negative part of the line in the x axis. This graph passes through the points $(0, 2)$ and $(2, 0)$.

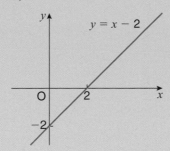

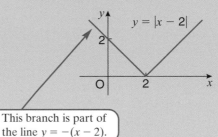

This branch is part of the line $y = -(x - 2)$.

A ADVICE

Remember that when you sketch a graph, you should show the co-ordinates of the points where the graph cuts the co-ordinate axes.

Equations involving a modulus sign

EXAMPLE 3

i) Use algebra to solve the equation $|x - 2| = 3$.
ii) Sketch a graph to illustrate your answer.

SOLUTION

i) $|x - 2| = 3$
$\Rightarrow x - 2 = 3$ or $x - 2 = -3$
$\quad x = 5 \qquad\qquad x = -1$
The roots are $x = 5$ and $x = -1$.

ii)

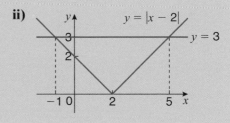

A ADVICE

If the right-hand side of the equation is anything other than a simple number, you should always start by drawing a graph.

EXAMPLE 4

i) Sketch the graph of $y = |2x + 1|$.
ii) Add the graph of $y = 3x + 4$ to your sketch, and hence solve the equation $|2x + 1| = 3x + 4$.

SOLUTION

i) Start by sketching the graph of $y = 2x + 1$. This graph passes through the points $(0, 1)$ and $(-\frac{1}{2}, 0)$.

Now reflect the negative part of the graph in the x axis.

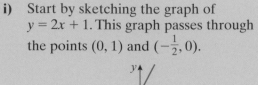

ii)

> This branch is $y = -2x - 1$.

> This point is the intersection of the lines $y = -2x - 1$ and $y = 3x + 4$.

$y = |2x + 1|$

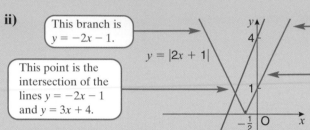

> This branch is $y = 2x + 1$.

> There is no intersection point of the lines $y = 2x + 1$ and $y = 3x + 4$, since the blue line is steeper than the red one.

$y = 3x + 4$

There is only one root. It is given by $-2x - 1 = 3x + 4$

$$-5 = 5x$$

$$x = -1$$

Example 4 illustrates how important it is to draw a graph and to use it to decide how many roots there are. Without a graph you might think you can find another root by solving $2x + 1 = 3x + 4$, which gives $x = -3$, but you would be wrong. It is on the negative part of the line $y = 2x + 1$.

Inequalities involving a modulus sign

Look at the graph below, which shows the graphs of $y = |x|$ and $y = 2$.

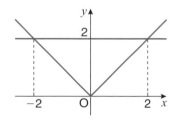

The solution to the inequality $|x| < 2$ is the set of values of x for which the red line lies below the blue line. This is given by $-2 < x < 2$.

The solution to the inequality $|x| > 2$ is the set of values of x for which the red line lies above the blue line. There are two parts to this solution: $x < -2$ and $x > 2$.

You can use these ideas to solve inequalities algebraically, if the right-hand side of the inequality is just a number.

EXAMPLE 5 Solve the inequalities

i) $|x - 3| < 1$ **ii)** $|2x + 1| \geqslant 3$

SOLUTION

i) $|x - 3| < 1 \quad \Rightarrow \quad -1 < x - 3 < 1$
$\qquad\qquad\qquad\qquad\quad 2 < x < 4$

ii) $|2x + 1| \geqslant 3 \quad \Rightarrow \quad 2x + 1 \leqslant -3 \quad \text{or} \quad 2x + 1 \geqslant 3$
$\qquad\qquad\qquad\qquad\qquad 2x \leqslant -4 \qquad\qquad\quad 2x \geqslant 2$
$\qquad\qquad\qquad\qquad\qquad\; x \leqslant -2 \qquad\qquad\qquad x \geqslant 1$

If the right-hand side of the inequality is not just a simple number, you must always start by drawing a sketch graph.

EXAMPLE 6

Solve the inequality $|3x - 2| < x + 1$.

SOLUTION

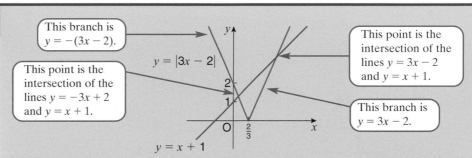

This branch is $y = -(3x - 2)$.

This point is the intersection of the lines $y = -3x + 2$ and $y = x + 1$.

$y = |3x - 2|$

$y = x + 1$

This point is the intersection of the lines $y = 3x - 2$ and $y = x + 1$.

This branch is $y = 3x - 2$.

The solution of the inequality is the set of values of x for which the red graph lies below the blue graph.

The intersection points are $\quad -3x + 2 = x + 1 \quad$ and $\quad 3x - 2 = x + 1$
$\qquad\qquad\qquad\qquad\qquad\qquad 1 = 4x \qquad\qquad\qquad\qquad 2x = 3$
$\qquad\qquad\qquad\qquad\qquad\quad\; x = \frac{1}{4} \qquad\qquad\qquad\qquad x = \frac{3}{2}$

The solution of the inequality is $\frac{1}{4} < x < \frac{3}{2}$.

EXAMPLE 7

Write the inequality $-1 \leqslant x \leqslant 7$ in the form $|x - a| \leqslant b$.

SOLUTION

$|x - a| \leqslant b \quad \Rightarrow \quad -b \leqslant x - a \leqslant b$
$\qquad\qquad\qquad \Rightarrow \quad a - b \leqslant x \leqslant a + b$

Solving $a - b = -1$ and $a + b = 7$ simultaneously gives $a = 3$ and $b = 4$.

So $-1 \leqslant x \leqslant 7$ can be written as $|x - 3| \leqslant 4$.

LINKS

Pure Mathematics Inequalities involving the modulus function are used in the work on the Binomial Expansion (C4) and in work on Maclaurin Series (FP2).

Test Yourself

1 Which of the following could be the equation of the graph below?

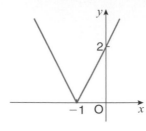

A $y = |2x + 1|$ B $y = 2|x| + 1$ C $y = |x| + 1$ D $y = 2|x + 1|$ E $y = |x| + 2$

2 Solve the inequality $|3x - 2| \geqslant 5$.

A $x \geqslant \dfrac{7}{3}$

B $x \geqslant \dfrac{7}{3}$ or $x \geqslant -1$

C $x \leqslant -1$ or $x \geqslant \dfrac{7}{3}$

D $-1 \leqslant x \leqslant \dfrac{7}{3}$

3 Solve the equation $3|x + 1| = 2x + 5$.

A $x = -\dfrac{8}{5}$ or $x = 2$

B $x = 2$ C $x = 4$

D $x = -\dfrac{4}{5}$ or $x = 4$

E $x = -\dfrac{2}{5}$ or $x = 2$

4 Write the inequality $-5 < x < 4$ in the form $|x - a| < b$.

A $|x - 0.5| < 4.5$

B $|x - 4.5| < -0.5$

C $|x + 4.5| < -0.5$

D $|x + 0.5| < 4.5$

5 Solve the inequality $|x - 2| > 2x - 1$.

A $x > 1$ B $x < 1$ C $x < -1$ D $-1 < x < 1$

Exam-Style Question

i)   Sketch the graph of $y = |2x - 1|$.

ii) Solve the inequality $|2x - 1| \leqslant 3x + 2$.

Differentiation

Product and quotient rules

A ABOUT THIS TOPIC

Sometimes you need to differentiate the product of two functions. For example, $\sin x \, e^{2x}$ is the product of the function $u(x) = e^{2x}$ and $v(x) = \sin x$. The product rule allows you to do this.

At other times you need to differentiate the quotient of two functions, $\dfrac{u(x)}{v(x)}$, for example $\dfrac{3x}{\ln(x-7)}$, and the quotient rule allows you to do this.

R REMEMBER

- The derivative of x^n from C1.
- Trigonometric identities from C2.
- The derivatives of $\ln x$, e^x and trigonometric functions from C3.
- The chain rule from C3.

K KEY FACTS

- Product rule:
  If $y = uv$, where the variables u and v both are functions of x,

  then $\dfrac{dy}{dx} = u\dfrac{dv}{dx} + v\dfrac{du}{dx}$.

- Quotient rule:
  If $y = \dfrac{u}{v}$, where the variables u and v both are functions of x,

  then $\dfrac{dy}{dx} = \dfrac{v\dfrac{du}{dx} - u\dfrac{dv}{dx}}{v^2}$.

If you need to differentiate the product of two functions, use the product rule as in the next two examples.

EXAMPLE 1 Use the product rule to differentiate $y = 3x \sin x$.

SOLUTION

$y = 3x \sin x$

Let $u = 3x$ and $v = \sin x$

$\dfrac{du}{dx} = 3 \qquad \dfrac{dv}{dx} = \cos x$

> Remember that the derivative of $\sin x$ is $\cos x$.

The product rule states that $\qquad y = uv$

$\Rightarrow \quad \dfrac{dy}{dx} = u\dfrac{dv}{dx} + v\dfrac{du}{dx}$

Substituting for u and v gives $\quad \dfrac{dy}{dx} = 3x \times \cos x + \sin x \times 3$

$\dfrac{dy}{dx} = 3(x \cos x + \sin x)$

> Notice that 3 is a common factor, so you can factorise.

When you use the product rule you can expect to have to do some algebra to tidy up the answer, as in the next example.

EXAMPLE 2

For $y = x\sqrt{3x - 2}$, find $\dfrac{dy}{dx}$.

SOLUTION

$y = x\sqrt{3x - 2}$

y is the product of two functions, x and $\sqrt{3x - 2}$. So you need to use the product rule.

Let $\quad u = x \quad$ and $\quad v = (3x - 2)^{\frac{1}{2}}$

$\dfrac{du}{dx} = 1 \qquad \dfrac{dv}{dx} = \dfrac{1}{2}(3x - 2)^{-\frac{1}{2}} \times 3$

> Use the chain rule to differentiate $(3x - 2)^{\frac{1}{2}}$

$\qquad\qquad\qquad \dfrac{dv}{dx} = \dfrac{3}{2}(3x - 2)^{-\frac{1}{2}}$

The product rule states that

$$y = uv$$

$$\Rightarrow \quad \dfrac{dy}{dx} = u\dfrac{dv}{dx} + v\dfrac{du}{dx}$$

Substituting for u and v gives $\quad \dfrac{dy}{dx} = x \times \dfrac{3}{2}(3x - 2)^{-\frac{1}{2}} + (3x - 2)^{\frac{1}{2}} \times 1$

$$\dfrac{dy}{dx} = \dfrac{3x}{2} \times \dfrac{1}{\sqrt{3x - 2}} + \sqrt{3x - 2}$$

$$\dfrac{dy}{dx} = \dfrac{3x}{2\sqrt{3x - 2}} + \sqrt{3x - 2}$$

This is the answer but you can tidy it up further to get

$$\dfrac{dy}{dx} = \dfrac{(9x - 4)\sqrt{3x - 2}}{2(3x - 2)}$$

If you need to differentiate the quotient of two functions, use the quotient rule, as in the next two examples.

EXAMPLE 3

Differentiate $y = \dfrac{4x - 1}{4 + 3x}$.

SOLUTION

y is a quotient of two functions, $(4x - 1)$ and $(4 + 3x)$. So you need to use the quotient rule.

$y = \dfrac{4x - 1}{4 + 3x}$

This is of the form $y = \dfrac{u}{v}$

So let $\quad u = 4x - 1 \quad$ and $\quad v = 4 + 3x$

$\qquad\quad \dfrac{du}{dx} = 4 \qquad\qquad\quad \dfrac{dv}{dx} = 3$

The quotient rule states that

$$y = \frac{u}{v} \quad \Rightarrow \quad \frac{dy}{dx} = \frac{v\frac{du}{dx} - u\frac{dv}{dx}}{v^2}$$

Substituting for u and v gives

$$\frac{dy}{dx} = \frac{(4 + 3x) \times 4 - (4x - 1) \times 3}{(4 + 3x)^2}$$

$$\frac{dy}{dx} = \frac{16 + 12x - 12x + 3}{(4 + 3x)^2}$$

$$\frac{dy}{dx} = \frac{19}{(4 + 3x)^2}$$

EXAMPLE 4

A curve has equation $y = \dfrac{x^3 + 1}{3x - 1}$.

i) Find $\dfrac{dy}{dx}$.

ii) Find the gradient of the curve at $(2, 5)$.

SOLUTION

i) $y = \dfrac{x^3 + 1}{3x - 1}$

This is of the form $y = \dfrac{u}{v}$ so use the quotient rule to differentiate it.

Let $\quad u = x^3 + 1 \quad$ and $\quad v = 3x - 1$

$$\frac{du}{dx} = 3x^2 \qquad \frac{dv}{dx} = 3$$

The quotient rule states that

$$y = \frac{u}{v} \quad \Rightarrow \quad \frac{dy}{dx} = \frac{v\frac{du}{dx} - u\frac{dv}{dx}}{v^2}$$

Substituting for u and v gives

$$\frac{dy}{dx} = \frac{(3x - 1) \times 3x^2 - (x^3 + 1) \times 3}{(3x - 1)^2}$$

$$\frac{dy}{dx} = \frac{9x^3 - 3x^2 - 3x^3 - 3}{(3x - 1)^2}$$

$$\frac{dy}{dx} = \frac{3(2x^3 - x^2 - 1)}{(3x - 1)^2}$$

ii) The gradient of the curve at $(2, 5)$ is the value of $\dfrac{dy}{dx}$ when $x = 2$.

Substituting $x = 2$ in $\dfrac{dy}{dx} = \dfrac{3(2x^3 - x^2 - 1)}{(3x - 1)^2} \quad \Rightarrow \quad \dfrac{dy}{dx} = \dfrac{33}{25} = 1.32$

4 Differentiation

EXAMPLE 5

Differentiate the following with respect to x:

i) $y = x^2 e^{3x}$

ii) $y = \dfrac{\ln x}{3x^2}$

SOLUTION

i) $y = x^2 e^{3x}$ This is of the form $y = uv$.

So you will use the product rule to differentiate it.

Let $u = x^2$ and $v = e^{3x}$

$\dfrac{du}{dx} = 2x$ $\dfrac{dv}{dx} = 3e^{3x}$ ◄

> Remember that the derivative of e^{ax} is ae^{ax}.

The product rule states that for $y = uv$, $\dfrac{dy}{dx} = u\dfrac{dv}{dx} + v\dfrac{du}{dx}$

Substituting for u and v gives

$\dfrac{dy}{dx} = x^2 \times 3e^{3x} + e^{3x} \times 2x$

$= e^{3x}(3x^2 + 2x)$

$= x(3x + 2)e^{3x}$

> Notice that x and e^{3x} are common factors.

ii) $y = \dfrac{\ln x}{3x^2}$

This is of the form $y = \dfrac{u}{v}$ so use the quotient rule.

Let $u = \ln x$ and $v = 3x^2$

$\dfrac{du}{dx} = \dfrac{1}{x}$ $\dfrac{dv}{dx} = 6x$

The quotient rule states that

$$y = \dfrac{u}{v} \quad \Rightarrow \quad \dfrac{dy}{dx} = \dfrac{v\dfrac{du}{dx} - u\dfrac{dv}{dx}}{v^2}$$

Substituting for u and v gives $\dfrac{dy}{dx} = \dfrac{3x^2 \times \dfrac{1}{x} - \ln x \times 6x}{(3x^2)^2}$

$\dfrac{dy}{dx} = \dfrac{3x - 6x \ln x}{9x^4}$

Factorising $\dfrac{dy}{dx} = \dfrac{3x(1 - 2\ln x)}{9x^4}$

$\dfrac{dy}{dx} = \dfrac{1 - 2\ln x}{3x^3}$

LINKS

Pure Mathematics   Solution of Differential Equations (C4, DE and FP3), Integration (C3 and C4).

Statistics   Probability Density Functions (S3).

Test Yourself

1 The graph shows a part of the curve $y = x \sin 3x$. M is a maximum point.
  Four of the following statements are false and one is true.
  Which one is true?

  A The gradient at the point P is exactly -3.

  B The x co-ordinate of M is between 0.5 and 0.6.

  C When $x = \dfrac{\pi}{6}$, the gradient of the curve is $\dfrac{\pi}{2}$.

  D The line $y = x$ touches the curve between $x = 0$ and $x = \dfrac{\pi}{2}$.

  E To the right of the point P, the gradient of $y = x \sin 3x$ is always negative.

2 Which of the following is the derivative of the function $y = x^3 \ln\left(\dfrac{1}{x}\right)$?

  A $3x^2 \ln\left(\dfrac{1}{x}\right) - x$ 	 B $x^2\left(3 \ln\left(\dfrac{1}{x}\right) - 1\right)$ 	 C $x^2\left(3 \ln\left(\dfrac{1}{x}\right) + 1\right)$ 	 D $-3x$

3 The equation of a curve is $y = \dfrac{x}{2x + 1}$. Three of the following statements are false and one is true.
  Which one is true?

  A The gradient function is $\dfrac{\mathrm{d}y}{\mathrm{d}x} = \dfrac{1}{2}$.

  B The gradient function is positive for all values of x.

  C The gradient at $x = 2$ is $\dfrac{1}{25}$.

  D The gradient at $x = -2$ is $-\dfrac{1}{9}$.

4 Given that $y = \dfrac{x}{2 + 3 \ln x}$, find the value of $\dfrac{\mathrm{d}y}{\mathrm{d}x}$ when $x = 1$.

  A $-\dfrac{1}{4}$ 	 B $\dfrac{1}{2}$ 	 C $\dfrac{1}{4}$ 	 D $\dfrac{1}{3}$

5 Find the gradient of the curve $y = \dfrac{\cos 2x}{x}$ at the point where $x = \pi$.

  A $-\dfrac{2}{\pi}$ 	 B $-\dfrac{1}{\pi^2}$ 	 C $\dfrac{1}{\pi^2}$ 	 D 1

Exam-Style Question

A curve has equation $y = (x + 2)\mathrm{e}^{-x}$.

i)   Find the co-ordinates of the points where the curve cuts the axes.

ii) Find the co-ordinates of the stationary point, S, on the curve.

iii) By evaluating $\dfrac{\mathrm{d}^2y}{\mathrm{d}x^2}$ at S, determine whether the stationary point is a maximum or a minimum.

iv) Sketch the curve.
     You may use the result that $x\mathrm{e}^{-x} \to 0$ as $x \to \infty$.

Chain rule

You will often need to differentiate composite functions such as $(4x + 7)^8$, $\sqrt{7x - 4}$, $\ln(3x^2 + 2)$, e^{2x-1} and so on. You can do this using the chain rule; you may like to think of it as the function of a function rule.

- The derivative of x^n from C1.
- The derivatives of $\ln x$, e^x from C3.
- How to find the stationary points of a curve and to use them when you sketch it, from C1, C2.

- Chain rule:
$$\frac{dy}{dx} = \frac{dy}{du} \times \frac{du}{dx}$$

- Differentiating the logarithm of a function:

  If $\quad y = \ln[f(x)] \quad$ then $\quad \dfrac{dy}{dx} = \dfrac{f'(x)}{f(x)}$.

- Differentiating the exponential of a function:

  If $\quad y = e^{f(x)} \quad$ then $\quad \dfrac{dy}{dx} = f'(x)\, e^{f(x)}$.

- You will often use the chain rule to find the rate at which a quantity is changing with time, for example

  for $A = \pi r^2$
$$\frac{dA}{dt} = \frac{dA}{dr} \times \frac{dr}{dt} = 2\pi r \frac{dr}{dt}$$

Differentiating composite functions

The chain rule allows you to differentiate expressions that are a function of a function. You usually start by substituting u for the inside function, as in the following examples.

EXAMPLE 1   Differentiate $y = (4x - 5)^5$ by using the chain rule.

SOLUTION

$y = (4x - 5)^5$

Let $\qquad u = 4x - 5 \quad \Rightarrow \quad y = u^5$

$\qquad \dfrac{du}{dx} = 4 \qquad\qquad \dfrac{dy}{du} = 5u^4$

Chain rule $\quad \dfrac{dy}{dx} = \dfrac{dy}{du} \times \dfrac{du}{dx}$

$\qquad\qquad = 5u^4 \times 4$

$\qquad\qquad = 20(4x - 5)^4 \quad \longleftarrow$ Remember to substitute $u = 4x - 5$.

A ADVICE

With experience you can do a question like this in your head. That is fine but only when you are certain you will get it right. Until then write it out in full, as here.

EXAMPLE 2

For $y = \sqrt{6x + 2}$ find $\dfrac{dy}{dx}$.

SOLUTION

$y = \sqrt{6x + 2}$

Let $\qquad u = 6x + 2 \quad \Rightarrow \quad y = \sqrt{u} = u^{\frac{1}{2}}$

$\qquad \dfrac{du}{dx} = 6 \qquad\qquad \dfrac{dy}{du} = \dfrac{1}{2}u^{-\frac{1}{2}}$

Chain rule $\quad \dfrac{dy}{dx} = \dfrac{dy}{du} \times \dfrac{du}{dx}$

$\qquad \dfrac{dy}{dx} = \dfrac{1}{2}u^{-\frac{1}{2}} \times 6$

$\qquad \dfrac{du}{dx} = 3 \times (6x + 2)^{-\frac{1}{2}}$

$\qquad\qquad = \dfrac{3}{\sqrt{6x + 2}}$

EXAMPLE 3

Differentiate $y = \dfrac{1}{(4x^3 - x)^4}$.

SOLUTION

First write the function in the form $y = (4x^3 - x)^{-4}$.

Let $\qquad u = 4x^3 - x \quad \Rightarrow \quad y = u^{-4}$

$\qquad \dfrac{du}{dx} = 12x^2 - 1 \qquad \dfrac{dy}{du} = -4u^{-5}$

Chain rule $\quad \dfrac{dy}{dx} = \dfrac{dy}{du} \times \dfrac{du}{dx}$

$\qquad \dfrac{dy}{dx} = -4 \times (4x^3 - x)^{-5} \times (12x^2 - 1)$

$\qquad\qquad = -\dfrac{4(12x^2 - 1)}{(4x^3 - x)^5}$

EXAMPLE 4

Find the gradient of the curve $y = \dfrac{1}{(3x - 1)^2}$ at the point $\left(1, \frac{1}{4}\right)$.

4 Differentiation

SOLUTION

First write the function in the form $y = (3x - 1)^{-2}$.

Let $u = 3x - 1$ $\Rightarrow$ $y = u^{-2}$

$$\frac{du}{dx} = 3 \qquad\qquad \frac{dy}{du} = -2u^{-3}$$

Chain rule $\dfrac{dy}{dx} = \dfrac{dy}{du} \times \dfrac{du}{dx}$

$$\frac{dy}{dx} = -2u^{-3} \times 3$$
$$= -6 \times (3x - 1)^{-3}$$
$$= -\frac{6}{(3x - 1)^3}$$

Now you need to find $\dfrac{dy}{dx}$ at the point $\left(1, \frac{1}{4}\right)$.   ← You are finding the gradient at $\left(1, \frac{1}{4}\right)$.

Substituting $x = 1$ into $\dfrac{dy}{dx} = -\dfrac{6}{(3x - 1)^3}$

$$\frac{dy}{dx} = -\frac{3}{4}$$

The gradient is $-\dfrac{3}{4}$.

EXAMPLE 5

Differentiate $y = e^{3x^2 - 2}$ with respect to x.

SOLUTION

Let $u = 3x^2 - 2$ $\Rightarrow$ $y = e^u$

$$\frac{du}{dx} = 6x \qquad\qquad \frac{dy}{du} = e^u$$

Chain rule $\dfrac{dy}{dx} = \dfrac{dy}{du} \times \dfrac{du}{dx}$

$$\frac{dy}{dx} = e^u \times 6x$$
$$\frac{dy}{dx} = 6xe^{3x^2 - 2}$$

This result illustrates a general rule for differentiating exponentials.

If $y = e^{f(x)}$ then $\dfrac{dy}{dx} = f'(x)\, e^{f(x)}$.

EXAMPLE 6

Given that $y = \ln(x^3 - 4x)$, find $\dfrac{dy}{dx}$.

SOLUTION

Let $u = x^3 - 4x$ $\Rightarrow$ $y = \ln u$

$$\frac{du}{dx} = 3x^2 - 4 \qquad\qquad \frac{dy}{du} = \frac{1}{u}$$

$$\text{Chain rule} \quad \frac{\mathrm{d}y}{\mathrm{d}x} = \frac{\mathrm{d}y}{\mathrm{d}u} \times \frac{\mathrm{d}u}{\mathrm{d}x}$$

$$\frac{\mathrm{d}y}{\mathrm{d}x} = \frac{1}{u} \times (3x^2 - 4)$$

$$= \frac{3x^2 - 4}{x^3 - 4x}$$

This result illustrates a general rule for differentiating logarithms.

If $y = \ln[\mathrm{f}(x)]$ then $\dfrac{\mathrm{d}y}{\mathrm{d}x} = \dfrac{\mathrm{f}'(x)}{\mathrm{f}(x)}$.

Rates of change

The chain rule is often used in questions about rates of change, particularly with respect to time, as in the next example.

EXAMPLE 7

A culture of bacteria form a circle which increases in radius at a rate of 2 mm per hour. Find the rate at which the area is increasing when the radius is 20 mm.

SOLUTION

Denote the radius of a circle at the time t hours by r mm.

Then the area $A = \pi r^2$ mm².

You know that $\dfrac{\mathrm{d}r}{\mathrm{d}t} = 2$ mm per hour

and you are asked to find $\dfrac{\mathrm{d}A}{\mathrm{d}t}$ when $r = 20$.

> This is the rate at which the radius is increasing.

Using the chain rule $\dfrac{\mathrm{d}A}{\mathrm{d}t} = \dfrac{\mathrm{d}A}{\mathrm{d}r} \times \dfrac{\mathrm{d}r}{\mathrm{d}t}$

$$A = \pi r^2 \quad \Rightarrow \quad \frac{\mathrm{d}A}{\mathrm{d}r} = 2\pi r$$

So $\dfrac{\mathrm{d}A}{\mathrm{d}t} = 2\pi r \times \dfrac{\mathrm{d}r}{\mathrm{d}t}$

Substituting $r = 20$ and $\dfrac{\mathrm{d}r}{\mathrm{d}t} = 2$ gives

$$\frac{\mathrm{d}A}{\mathrm{d}r} = 2 \times \pi \times 20 \times 2 = 80\pi$$

So the area is increasing at 80π mm² per hour.

LINKS

Pure Mathematics	C4, FP2, FP3.
Differential Equations	DE.
Mechanics	M3, M4.
Statistics	Probability Density Functions (S3), Generating Functions (S4).

Test Yourself

1 Find the derivative of $y = (2x^2 - 3)^3$.

    A $3(2x^2 - 3)^2$ B $12x(2x^2 - 3)^3$ C $12x(2x^2 - 3)^2$ D $6x(2x^2 - 3)^2$

2 You are given that $y = \dfrac{1}{(1 - 2x)^3}$. Find $\dfrac{dy}{dx}$.

    A $-\dfrac{3}{(1 - 2x)^4}$ B $\dfrac{6}{(1 - 2x)^4}$ C $\dfrac{6}{(1 - 2x)^2}$ D $-\dfrac{6}{(1 - 2x)^4}$ E $\dfrac{6}{(1 - 2x)^3}$

3 Three of the following statements about the function $y = \sqrt{x^2 - 4x + 3}$ are false and one is true. Which one is true?

    A $\dfrac{dy}{dx} = \dfrac{2(x - 2)}{\sqrt{x^2 - 4x + 3}}$

    B The curve with equation $y = \sqrt{x^2 - 4x + 3}$ crosses the x axis at $(2, 0)$.

    C $y = \sqrt{x^2 - 4x + 3}$ is an increasing function.

    D Where the curve $y = \sqrt{x^2 - 4x + 3}$ crosses the y axis its gradient is $-\dfrac{2\sqrt{3}}{3}$.

4 You are given that $f(x) = 3 \ln (5x - 1)$. Find the exact value of $f'(2)$.

    A $\dfrac{1}{3}$ B $15 \ln 9$ C $\dfrac{5}{3}$ D 15

5 The diagram shows a cone which contains water to a depth h.

The half angle, α, of this cone is $\arctan \frac{1}{2}$ and so the volume of water is given by $V = \dfrac{\pi}{12}h^3$.

Water is poured into the cone at a steady rate of $5 \text{ cm}^3 \text{ s}^{-1}$.

At what rate is the depth increasing when $h = 10 \text{ cm}$?

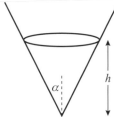

    A $125\pi \text{ cm s}^{-1}$ B $400\pi \text{ cm s}^{-1}$ C $5\pi \text{ cm s}^{-1}$ D $\dfrac{1}{5\pi} \text{ cm s}^{-1}$

Exam-Style Question

i)   Differentiate   A) $\sqrt{100 - x^2}$ B) $x\sqrt{100 - x^2}$

     The diagram shows a ladder of length 10 m leaning against a vertical wall. The foot of the ladder is on horizontal ground at a distance x m from the wall. The top of the ladder is at height h m. The area of the triangle formed by the ladder, the wall and the ground is A m^2.

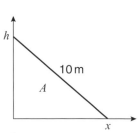

ii)   Show that $A = \frac{1}{2}x\sqrt{100 - x^2}$.

iii)   Show that the maximum possible value of A is 25.

iv)   The foot of the ladder slides away from the wall at a steady speed of 0.01 m s^{-1}. Find the rate at which the area is changing when $x = 6$.

Differentiating trigonometric functions

ABOUT THIS TOPIC

The trigonometric functions $y = \sin x$ and $y = \cos x$ are very important in Mathematics. Differentiation of these functions is used almost everywhere: Pure Mathematics, Mechanics, Numerical Methods.

R **REMEMBER**

- The gradient function $\dfrac{dy}{dx}$ from C1.
- Angles measured in radians from C2.
- Trigonometric functions and identities from C1, C2.
- The chain rule from C3.

K **KEY FACTS**

- When you are using calculus with trigonometric functions the angles must always be in radians.
- Standard results:

  If $y = \sin kx$ then $\dfrac{dy}{dx} = k \cos kx$.

  If $y = \cos kx$ then $\dfrac{dy}{dx} = -k \sin kx$.

  If $y = \tan kx$ then $\dfrac{dy}{dx} = \dfrac{k}{\cos^2 kx}$.

The standard results for differentiating $\sin kx$, $\cos kx$ and $\tan kx$ are given in the Key facts. Remember that the angles must be in radians.

The examples that follow use the results together with other techniques for differentiation, the chain rule, the product rule and the quotient rule.

EXAMPLE 1   Differentiate   **i)** $y = 10 + 8 \sin x$ **ii)** $y = x^5 + 3 \cos x$

SOLUTION

i) $y = 10 + 8 \sin x$

$\dfrac{dy}{dx} = 8 \cos x$

ii) $y = x^5 + 3 \cos x$

$\dfrac{dy}{dx} = 5x^4 - 3 \sin x$

EXAMPLE 2   Use the quotient rule to differentiate $y = \dfrac{\sin kx}{\cos kx}$.

SOLUTION   The quotient rule states that

If $y = \dfrac{u}{v}$, $\dfrac{dy}{dx} = \dfrac{v \dfrac{du}{dx} - u \dfrac{dv}{dx}}{v^2}$

Let $\quad u = \sin kx \quad \Rightarrow \quad \dfrac{du}{dx} = k \cos kx$

$\qquad v = \cos kx \quad \Rightarrow \quad \dfrac{dv}{dx} = -k \sin kx$

So $\quad \dfrac{dy}{dx} = \dfrac{\cos kx \times k \cos kx - \sin kx \times (-\sin kx)}{(\cos kx)^2}$

$\qquad\qquad = \dfrac{k \cos^2 x + k \sin^2 x}{\cos^2 kx}$

$\qquad\qquad = \dfrac{k (\cos^2 x + \sin^2 x)}{\cos^2 kx} \quad \longleftarrow \quad \boxed{\cos^2 kx + \sin^2 kx = 1}$

$\qquad\qquad = \dfrac{k}{\cos^2 kx}$

A ADVICE

Notice that $\dfrac{\sin kx}{\cos kx}$ is $\tan kx$, so you have differentiated $y = \tan kx$, getting the standard result

$\dfrac{dy}{dx} = \dfrac{k}{\cos^2 kx}$. In C4 you meet the relationship $\sec x = \dfrac{1}{\cos x}$, so in this case $\dfrac{dy}{dx}$ may also be written

as $k \sec^2 kx$.

EXAMPLE 3

Use the chain rule to differentiate the following functions with respect to x:

i) $\quad y = \sin (3x + \pi)$ $\qquad$ **ii)** $\quad y = \cos 4x^2$

SOLUTION

i) $\quad y = \sin (3x + \pi)$

$\qquad$ Let $\quad u = 3x + \pi \quad \Rightarrow \quad y = \sin u$

$\qquad\qquad \dfrac{du}{dx} = 3 \qquad\qquad \dfrac{dy}{du} = \cos u$

$\qquad$ Chain rule $\quad \dfrac{dy}{dx} = \dfrac{dy}{du} \times \dfrac{du}{dx}$

$\qquad\qquad\qquad\quad \dfrac{dy}{dx} = \cos u \times 3$

$\qquad\qquad\qquad\quad \dfrac{dy}{dx} = 3 \cos (3x + \pi)$

ii) $\quad y = \cos 4x^2$

$\qquad$ Let $\quad u = 4x^2 \quad \Rightarrow \quad y = \cos u$

$\qquad\qquad \dfrac{du}{dx} = 8x \qquad\qquad \dfrac{dy}{du} = -\sin u$

$\qquad$ Chain rule $\quad \dfrac{dy}{dx} = \dfrac{dy}{du} \times \dfrac{du}{dx}$

$\qquad\qquad\qquad\quad \dfrac{dy}{dx} = -\sin u \times 8x$

$\qquad\qquad\qquad\quad \dfrac{dy}{dx} = -8x \sin 4x^2$

EXAMPLE 4

Differentiate $y = \cos^2 x$

i) using the chain rule   **ii)** using the product rule.

SOLUTION

i) $y = \cos^2 x$ ⟵

> $y = \cos^2 x$ means $y = (\cos x)^2$.

Let $u = \cos x$ $\Rightarrow$ $y = u^2$

$$\frac{du}{dx} = -\sin x \qquad \frac{dy}{du} = 2u$$

Chain rule $\dfrac{dy}{dx} = \dfrac{dy}{du} \times \dfrac{du}{dx}$

$$\frac{dy}{dx} = 2u \times (-\sin x)$$

$$\frac{dy}{dx} = -2\cos x \sin x$$

ii) $y = \cos^2 x = \cos x \times \cos x$

Product rule $y = u \times v$ $\Rightarrow$ $\dfrac{dy}{dx} = v\dfrac{du}{dx} + u\dfrac{dv}{dx}$

Let $u = \cos x$ and $v = \cos x$

$$\frac{du}{dx} = -\sin x \qquad \frac{dv}{dx} = -\sin x$$

$$\frac{dy}{dx} = \cos x \times (-\sin x) + \cos x \times (-\sin x)$$

$$\frac{dy}{dx} = -2\cos x \sin x$$

> As you would expect, you get the same result for $\dfrac{dy}{dx}$ whether you use the chain rule or the product rule.

You will often meet questions about the graphs of equations that involve trigonometric functions, as in the next example.

EXAMPLE 5

The graph shows part of the curve $y = x + \cos 2x$.

Find the co-ordinates of the points P and Q to 2 decimal places.

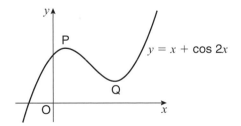

SOLUTION

P is a maximum point and Q is a minimum point so, at both P and Q,
$\dfrac{dy}{dx} = 0$.

$$y = x + \cos 2x \qquad \Rightarrow \qquad \frac{dy}{dx} = 1 - 2\sin 2x$$

Solving $1 - 2\sin 2x = 0$

gives $\sin 2x = \dfrac{1}{2}$ $\Rightarrow$ $2x = \dfrac{\pi}{6}, \dfrac{5\pi}{6}, \ldots$

4 Differentiation

So $\qquad x = \dfrac{\pi}{12}, \dfrac{5\pi}{12}, \ldots$

So at P, $\quad x = \dfrac{\pi}{12} \quad \Rightarrow \quad y = \dfrac{\pi}{12} + \cos\dfrac{\pi}{6} = 1.13$ (to 2 d.p.)

at Q, $\qquad x = \dfrac{5\pi}{12} \quad \Rightarrow \quad y = \dfrac{5\pi}{12} + \cos\dfrac{5\pi}{6} = 0.44$ (to 2 d.p.)

P is $(0.26, 1.13)$ and Q is $(1.31, 0.44)$. ◄

> $\dfrac{\pi}{12} = 0.26$
> to 2 d.p.
> $\dfrac{5\pi}{12} = 1.31$
> to 2 d.p.

LINKS

Pure Mathematics   Solution of Differential Equations (C4, DE and FP3).
Mechanics   Simple Harmonic Motion (M3).
Differential Equations   Throughout but particularly Second Order Differential
Equations (DE) and Oscillations (DE).

Test Yourself

1 Find $\dfrac{dy}{dx}$, given that $y = 2\cos 3x + 5$.

   A $6\sin 3x$ **B** $-2\sin 3x$ **C** $-\dfrac{2}{3}\sin 3x$ **D** $-6\sin 3x$ **E** $-6\sin 3x + 5$

2 The graph shows part of the curve $y = \sin x + \cos x$.

Three of the following statements are false and one is true.
Which one is true?

   A At the point P, $x = \dfrac{\pi}{2}$.   **B** The gradient at Q is 2.

   C At R the value of y is -1.

   D The gradient of the curve always lies between a minimum
value of $-\sqrt{2}$ and a maximum value of $\sqrt{2}$.

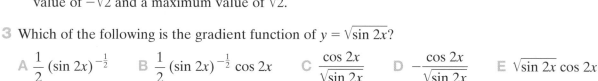

3 Which of the following is the gradient function of $y = \sqrt{\sin 2x}$?

   A $\dfrac{1}{2}(\sin 2x)^{-\frac{1}{2}}$ **B** $\dfrac{1}{2}(\sin 2x)^{-\frac{1}{2}}\cos 2x$ **C** $\dfrac{\cos 2x}{\sqrt{\sin 2x}}$ **D** $-\dfrac{\cos 2x}{\sqrt{\sin 2x}}$ **E** $\sqrt{\sin 2x}\cos 2x$

4 You are given the equation of a curve $y = \ln\left(\cos\dfrac{x}{2}\right)$. Which of the following is true?

   A $\dfrac{dy}{dx} = \dfrac{1}{2}\tan\dfrac{x}{2}$ **B** $\dfrac{dy}{dx} = -\dfrac{1}{2}\tan\dfrac{x}{2}$ **C** $\dfrac{dy}{dx} = -\dfrac{1}{2}\cos\dfrac{x}{2}\sin\dfrac{x}{2}$ **D** $\dfrac{dy}{dx} = -\tan\dfrac{x}{2}$

Exam-Style Question

You are given that $y = 5\sin\theta - 4\cos\theta$.

i) Find $\dfrac{dy}{d\theta}$.

ii) Find the co-ordinates of the stationary points for $-\pi \leqslant \theta \leqslant \pi$.

iii) Find $\dfrac{d^2y}{d\theta^2}$ and hence determine whether each of the stationary points is a maximum, a minimum
or a point of inflection.

iv) Sketch the graph of y against θ for $-\pi \leqslant \theta \leqslant \pi$.

Implicit differentiation

A **ABOUT THIS TOPIC**

Here you will learn how to differentiate a function which has not been given explicitly in the form $y = f(x)$, that is, in terms of the independent variable. An example of this is $e^{2y} = x^2 + y$. Here y is a function of the independent variable x, defined implicitly by the equation. This topic deals with finding $\dfrac{dy}{dx}$ in this situation. You will also learn about the relationship between $\dfrac{dy}{dx}$ and $\dfrac{dx}{dy}$.

R **REMEMBER**

- Differentiation from C1 and C2.
- Differentiation of trigonometric, exponential and logarithmic functions from C3.
- Composition of functions from C3.
- Inverse functions from C3.
- The product rule, quotient rule and chain rule for differentiation from C3.

K **KEY FACTS**

- If you differentiate y^5 with respect to y, you get $5y^4$.
- If you differentiate y^5 with respect to x, you get $5y^4 \dfrac{dy}{dx}$.

- If y is a function of x then $\dfrac{dx}{dy} = \dfrac{1}{\dfrac{dy}{dx}}$.

Implicit differentiation

The chain rule is needed to differentiate implicit functions. Suppose you are asked to differentiate y^5 with respect to x. You know that if you differentiate it with respect to y, the answer is $5y^4$ but that is not what you were asked to do. To see how to do it, it is helpful to use a letter to denote y^5, say z.

Let $z = y^5$ so $\dfrac{dz}{dy} = 5y^4$. Now apply the chain rule in the form

$$\frac{dz}{dx} = \frac{dz}{dy} \frac{dy}{dx}$$

$$\frac{dz}{dx} = 5y^4 \frac{dy}{dx}$$

This is the answer. You will notice that you could have just written this answer down. There are two parts multiplied together.

- $5y^4$ is the derivative of y^5 with respect to y.

- $\dfrac{dy}{dx}$ allows for the fact that you are differentiating with respect to x, not y.

This is called implicit differentiation.

EXAMPLE 1

In each case differentiate the expression given with respect to x.

i) y^3 **ii)** $\ln y$ **iii)** $\sin(4y)$.

SOLUTION

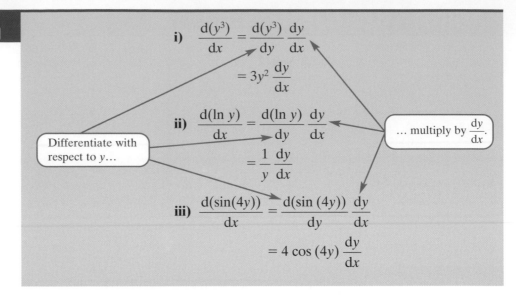

i) $\dfrac{d(y^3)}{dx} = \dfrac{d(y^3)}{dy}\dfrac{dy}{dx}$

$\qquad\qquad = 3y^2 \dfrac{dy}{dx}$

ii) $\dfrac{d(\ln y)}{dx} = \dfrac{d(\ln y)}{dy}\dfrac{dy}{dx}$

$\qquad\qquad = \dfrac{1}{y}\dfrac{dy}{dx}$

iii) $\dfrac{d(\sin(4y))}{dx} = \dfrac{d(\sin(4y))}{dy}\dfrac{dy}{dx}$

$\qquad\qquad = 4\cos(4y)\dfrac{dy}{dx}$

Differentiate with respect to y…

… multiply by $\dfrac{dy}{dx}$.

Sometimes you will need to use the product and quotient rules, as in the next two examples.

EXAMPLE 2

Differentiate y^2x^3 with respect to x.

SOLUTION

The question involves a product so the product rule is needed.

Let $u = y^2$ and $v = x^3$ so that $\dfrac{du}{dx} = 2y\dfrac{dy}{dx}$ and $\dfrac{dv}{dx} = 3x^2$.

By the product rule the answer is

$$u\dfrac{dv}{dx} + v\dfrac{du}{dx} = y^2 \times 3x^2 + x^3 \times 2y\dfrac{dy}{dx} = x^2y\left(3y + 2x\dfrac{dy}{dx}\right)$$

EXAMPLE 3

Differentiate $\dfrac{\sin y}{e^x}$ with respect to x.

SOLUTION

This question involves a quotient so the quotient rule is needed.

Let $u = \sin y$ and $v = e^x$ so that $\dfrac{du}{dx} = \cos y\dfrac{dy}{dx}$ and $\dfrac{dv}{dx} = e^x$.

By the quotient rule the answer is

$$\dfrac{v\dfrac{du}{dx} - u\dfrac{dv}{dx}}{v^2} = \dfrac{e^x \times \cos y\dfrac{dy}{dx} - \sin y \times e^x}{(e^x)^2}$$

$$= \dfrac{\cos y\dfrac{dy}{dx} - \sin y}{e^x}$$

$u = \sin y$ so

$\dfrac{du}{dx} = \dfrac{d(\sin y)}{dx}$

$\qquad = \dfrac{d(\sin y)}{dy}\dfrac{dy}{dx}$

$\qquad = \cos y\dfrac{dy}{dx}$

You will meet questions, like that in the next example, where $\dfrac{dy}{dx}$ occurs more than once after you have differentiated. In such cases you need to collect all the $\dfrac{dy}{dx}$ terms on one side and then factorise it.

EXAMPLE 4

Find $\dfrac{dy}{dx}$ if $e^{2y} = x^2 + y$. By differentiating with respect to y find $\dfrac{dx}{dy}$.

Comment on these results.

SOLUTION

Differentiating both sides of $e^{2y} = x^2 + y$ with respect to x gives

$$\frac{d(e^{2y})}{dx} = \frac{d(e^{2y})}{dy}\frac{dy}{dx}$$
$$= 2e^{2y}\frac{dy}{dx}$$

$$2e^{2y}\frac{dy}{dx} = 2x + \frac{dy}{dx}$$

$$\frac{d(y)}{dx} = \frac{d(y)}{dy}\frac{dy}{dx}$$
$$= 1 \times \frac{dy}{dx} = \frac{dy}{dx}$$

$$\Rightarrow \quad 2e^{2y}\frac{dy}{dx} - \frac{dy}{dx} = 2x$$

Make $\dfrac{dy}{dx}$ the subject of this equation.

$$\Rightarrow \quad \frac{dy}{dx}(2e^{2y} - 1) = 2x$$

$$\Rightarrow \quad \frac{dy}{dx} = \frac{2x}{2e^{2y} - 1}$$

Differentiating both sides of $e^{2y} = x^2 + y$ with respect to y gives

Here you are differentiating x^2 with respect to y. Differentiate it with respect to x and then multiply by $\dfrac{dx}{dy}$ to give $2x\dfrac{dx}{dy}$.

$$2e^{2y} = 2x\frac{dx}{dy} + 1$$

$$\Rightarrow \quad 2e^{2y} - 1 = 2x\frac{dx}{dy}$$

Make $\dfrac{dx}{dy}$ the subject of this equation.

$$\Rightarrow \quad \frac{dx}{dy} = \frac{2e^{2y} - 1}{2x}$$

It can be seen that $\dfrac{dx}{dy} = \dfrac{1}{\dfrac{dy}{dx}}$.

 $\dfrac{dx}{dy} = \dfrac{1}{\dfrac{dy}{dx}}$ is a general result that you need to know.

EXAMPLE 5

The curve shown is defined by the equation $3y^2 + y = 7x^2 + 2$.

i) Find $\dfrac{dy}{dx}$ and hence find the gradient of the curve at the point A (2, 3).

ii) Find the co-ordinates of points on the curve where $\dfrac{dy}{dx} = 0$.

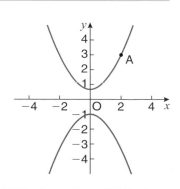

4 Differentiation

SOLUTION

i) Differentiating both sides of $3y^2 + y = 7x^2 + 2$ with respect to x gives

$$6y\frac{dy}{dx} + \frac{dy}{dx} = 14x$$

> Make $\dfrac{dy}{dx}$ the subject of this equation.

$$\Rightarrow \quad \frac{dy}{dx}(6y + 1) = 14x$$

$$\Rightarrow \quad \frac{dy}{dx} = \frac{14x}{6y + 1}$$

For the point $(2, 3)$, substitute $x = 2$, $y = 3$ into this: $\dfrac{dy}{dx} = \dfrac{28}{19}$.

ii) $\dfrac{dy}{dx} = 0$, so $\dfrac{14x}{6y + 1} = 0$. Therefore $x = 0$.

> $\dfrac{14x}{6y + 1} = 0$ only when $14x = 0$, i.e. $x = 0$.

Substitute $x = 0$ into $3y^2 + y = 7x^2 + 2$:

$$3y^2 + y = 2$$

$$\Rightarrow \quad 3y^2 + y - 2 = 0$$

$$\Rightarrow \quad (3y - 2)(y + 1) = 0$$

> Remember to find the y co-ordinates.

$$\Rightarrow \quad y = \tfrac{2}{3} \text{ or } y = -1$$

The points on the curve where $\dfrac{dy}{dx} = 0$ are $\left(0, \tfrac{2}{3}\right)$ and $(0, -1)$.

LINKS

Pure Mathematics	Differentiation (C2), Integration (C2), Calculus (FP2), Differential Geometry (FP3), Differential Equations (DE), Numerical Methods.
Mechanics	Volumes of Revolution and Centres of Mass (M3), Variable Force and Mass (M4).
Statistics	Probability Density Functions (S3).

Test Yourself

1 Differentiate y^2 with respect to x.

   A $2y$ B $2x$ C $y^2\dfrac{dy}{dx}$ D $2y\dfrac{dy}{dx}$

2 Differentiate $\cos y$ with respect to x.

   A $-\sin y$ B $-\sin y\dfrac{dy}{dx}$ C $\sin y\dfrac{dy}{dx}$ D $-\sin x$

3 Find $\dfrac{dy}{dx}$ when $y^2 = e^x + \sin y$.

   A $\dfrac{e^x}{2y - \cos y}$ B $\dfrac{e^x}{2y + \cos y}$ C $\dfrac{e^x + \cos y}{2y}$ D $\dfrac{2y - e^x}{\cos y}$

4 Find the gradient of the curve shown at the point $(2, 3)$.
   It is defined implicitly by the equation $y^2 + 2 = x^3 + y$.

   A $\dfrac{12}{5}$ B 9

   C 2   D -6

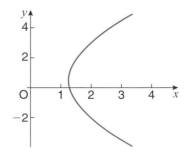

5 Find $\dfrac{dy}{dx}$ when $y^2 = ye^x + x^2$.

   A $\dfrac{ye^x + 2x}{2y + e^x}$ B $\dfrac{2x}{2y - e^x}$ C $\dfrac{ye^x + 2x}{2y - e^x}$ D $\dfrac{2x}{2y + e^x}$

Exam-Style Question

The diagram shows the curve that is defined implicitly by the equation
$y^3 = 2xy + x^2$.

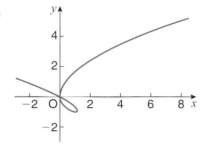

i)   Show that $\dfrac{dy}{dx} = \dfrac{2(x + y)}{3y^2 - 2x}$.

ii) Write down $\dfrac{dx}{dy}$ in terms of x and y. Show that A $(3, 3)$ is
     a point on the curve and find the value of $\dfrac{dx}{dy}$ at A.

iii) State, with a reason, whether the line $y = x$ is a tangent to the curve at $(3, 3)$.

Integration

Integration by substitution (including ln integrals)

A ABOUT THIS TOPIC

You should already know how to integrate negative and fractional powers from your work in C2. Not all expressions can be integrated (even if you have a maths degree!) but in this topic you will learn how to integrate some more complicated functions.

R REMEMBER

- Techniques for differentiation from C3.
- Integration from C2.
- $\int kx^n \, dx = \dfrac{kx^{n+1}}{n+1} + c$ where k and n are constants but $n \neq -1$.
- Laws of indices from C1.
- What a function of a function is from C3.
- Natural logarithms and exponentials from C3.
- Laws of logarithms from C2.

K KEY FACTS

- $\int e^x \, dx = e^x + c$ and $\int e^{ax} \, dx = \dfrac{1}{a} e^{ax} + c$

- $\int \dfrac{1}{x} \, dx = \ln|x| + c$

- $\int \dfrac{f'(x)}{f(x)} \, dx = \ln|f(x)| + c$

Some integrals which cannot be integrated directly can be transformed into a simpler form by using a substitution. You need to write one of the functions as u and then rewrite the whole integral (including the 'dx') in terms of u.

When an integral contains a 'function of a function' it usually helps to use a substitution for the 'inside' function.

For example, for $\int \sqrt{x-3} \, dx$ then $\sqrt{x-3}$ is a function ($\sqrt{}$) of a function $(x-3)$ so use $u = x - 3$.

 When faced with a function which you can't integrate by inspection, always check first that it doesn't simplify into one that you can!

EXAMPLE 1   Find $\int \sqrt{2x+5} \, dx$.

$\sqrt{2x+5}$ is a function of a function. You can't integrate it directly but you can use the substitution $u = 2x + 5$ to transform this integral into one you can do.

Let $u = 2x + 5$

You can't find $\int \sqrt{u} \, dx$ as you can't integrate u with respect to x so you need to convert the dx to du.

$$\frac{du}{dx} = 2 \Rightarrow du = 2 \, dx \Rightarrow \frac{1}{2} \, du = dx$$

> Take care with this rearrangement – it is a common cause of error!

Now substitute into the original integral.

$$\int \sqrt{2x+5} \, dx = \int \sqrt{u} \, \frac{1}{2} \, du$$

> Replace $2x + 5$ with u and dx with $\frac{1}{2} du$.

> Remember $\sqrt{u} = u^{\frac{1}{2}}$.

$$= \int \frac{1}{2} u^{\frac{1}{2}} \, du$$

$$= \frac{1}{2} \times \frac{2}{3} u^{\frac{3}{2}} + c$$

> Don't forget the '+ c'.

$$= \frac{1}{3} u^{\frac{3}{2}} + c$$

To get the final answer replace u with $2x + 5$.

So $\int \sqrt{2x+5} \, dx = \frac{1}{3}(2x+5)^{\frac{3}{2}} + c$

> ⚠ Don't forget to substitute back for x. Never leave your final answer in terms of u.

A ADVICE

This process is like the chain rule for differentiation in reverse.
With practice you can integrate functions like the one above by inspection.

When you have a definite integral you need to rewrite the limits before substituting them in.

EXAMPLE 2

Evaluate $\int_0^2 x(x^2 - 3)^5 \, dx$ by using the substitution $u = x^2 - 3$.

Let $u = x^2 - 3$

Convert dx to du

$$\frac{du}{dx} = 2x \Rightarrow du = 2x \, dx \Rightarrow \frac{1}{2} \, du = x \, dx$$

> You have an 'x' in the integral – so leave the 'x' with the 'dx' when you rearrange.

You need to convert the limits

$$x = 2 \Rightarrow u = 2^2 - 3 = 1$$

$$x = 0 \Rightarrow u = 0 - 3 = -3$$

Now substitute into the original integral

$$\int_0^2 x(x^2 - 3)^5 \, dx = \int_0^2 (x^2 - 3)^5 x \, dx$$

Replace $x^2 - 3$ with u and $x \, dx$ with $\frac{1}{2} \, du$ and change the limits.

$$= \int_{-3}^{1} u^5 \times \frac{1}{2} \, du$$

This is what you are aiming for: a function you can integrate directly.

$$= \left[\frac{1}{2} \times \frac{1}{6} u^6 \right]_{-3}^{1}$$

$$= \left(\frac{1}{12} \times 1^6 \right) - \left(\frac{1}{12} \times (-3)^6 \right)$$

$$= -60\tfrac{2}{3}$$

 You might have been tempted to use the binomial theorem to expand the brackets and then integrate term by term. In this case, this would work but it would be very time consuming and result in a long and messy answer.

You can use the fact that the derivative of e^x is e^x (from C3 Exponentials) and the fact that integration is the reverse of differentiation to say

$$\frac{d}{dx}(e^{ax}) = ae^{ax} \implies \int e^{ax} \, dx = \frac{1}{a} e^{ax} + c$$

EXAMPLE 3

Here is a sketch of the curve $y = 3x^2 e^{(1-x^3)}$.

Find the exact area of the shaded region.

Use the substitution $u = (1 - x^3)$.

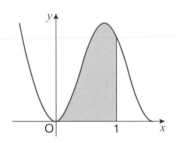

SOLUTION

You need to find $\int_0^1 3x^2 e^{(1-x^3)} \, dx$.

Let $u = 1 - x^3$

Convert dx to du

You can write $-du = 3x^2 \, dx$ as $-1 \, du = 3x^2 \, dx$.

$$\frac{du}{dx} = -3x^2 \implies du = -3x^2 \, dx \implies -du = 3x^2 \, dx$$

You need to convert the limits

$$x = 1 \implies u = 1 - 1^3 = 0$$
$$x = 0 \implies u = 1 - 0 = 1$$

Now substitute into the original integral

$$\int_0^1 3x^2 e^{(1-x^3)} \, dx = \int_1^0 e^{(1-x^3)} \times 3x^2 \, dx$$

Replace $(1 - x^3)$ with u and $3x^2 \, dx$ with $-1 \, du$ and change the limits.

Take extra care with the limits. The upper limit isn't always the larger number.

$$= \int_1^0 e^u \times -1 \, du$$

$$= \int_1^0 -e^u \, du$$

$$= \left[-e^u \right]_1^0$$

$$= (-e^0) - (-e^1)$$

$$= -1 + e$$

You were asked for the exact value so don't work this out.

$$= e - 1$$

You can use the fact that the derivative of $\ln x$ is $\dfrac{1}{x}$ (from C3 Exponentials)

and the fact that integration is the reverse of differentiation to say

$$\frac{d}{dx}(\ln x) = \frac{1}{x} \implies \int \frac{1}{x}\,dx = \ln|x| + c$$

Using this result and the technique of integration by substitution enables you to integrate some quotients.

EXAMPLE 4 Find $\displaystyle\int \frac{2x}{x^2+4}\,dx$.

SOLUTION

You can think of $\displaystyle\int \frac{2x}{x^2+4}\,dx$ as $\displaystyle\int \frac{1}{x^2+4} \times 2x\,dx$.

$\dfrac{1}{x^2+4}$ is a function of a function so use the substitution $u = x^2 + 4$.

Let $u = x^2 + 4$

Convert dx to du

$$\frac{du}{dx} = 2x \implies du = 2x\,dx$$

> Replace $x^2 + 4$ with u and $2x\,dx$ with du.

$$\int \frac{2x}{x^2+4}\,dx = \int \frac{1}{u}\,du$$

$$= \ln|u| + c$$

To get the final answer replace u with $x^2 + 4$.

So $\displaystyle\int \frac{2x}{x^2+4}\,dx = \ln(x^2+4) + c$

> You don't need the modulus signs as $x^2 + 4$ is always positive.

! Notice that in $\displaystyle\int \frac{2x}{x^2+4}\,dx$, the top line $(2x)$ is the derivative of the bottom line

$(x^2 + 4)$ and when you integrate you get an answer of $\ln|\text{bottom line}| + c$.
This leads to the useful result that

$$\int \frac{f'(x)}{f(x)}\,dx = \ln|f(x)| + c$$

With practice you can use inspection to integrate quotients which are in this form.

EXAMPLE 5 Evaluate $\displaystyle\int_{-2}^{0} \frac{6}{1-2x}\,dx$.

SOLUTION

The derivative of $1 - 2x$ is -2.

So you can adjust the top line to make it the derivative of the bottom line:

> You could use the substitution $u = 1 - 2x$ instead.

$$\int_{-2}^{0} \frac{6}{1-2x}\,dx = \int_{-2}^{0} \frac{-3 \times -2}{1-2x}\,dx = -3\int_{-2}^{0} \frac{-2}{1-2x}\,dx$$

> Since $-3 \times -2 = 6$, the integral is unchanged.

Now the top line is the derivative of the bottom line so you can use the rule

$$\int \frac{f'(x)}{f(x)}\, dx = \ln |f(x)| + c$$

$$\int_{-2}^{0} \frac{6}{1 - 2x}\, dx = -3 \int_{-2}^{0} \frac{-2}{1 - 2x}\, dx$$

$$= \left[-3 \ln |1 - 2x| \right]_{-2}^{0}$$

$$= (-3\ln 1^{=0}) - (-3 \ln 5)$$

$$= 3 \ln 5$$

> You may be able to go straight to this line but to avoid mistakes it is best to show all of your working.

LINKS

Pure Mathematics	Integration (C4), Calculus (FP2), Differential Geometry (FP3), Differential Equations (DE), Numerical Methods.
Mechanics	Volumes of Revolution and Centres of Mass (M3), Variable Force and Mass (M4).
Statistics	Probability Density Functions (S3).

Test Yourself

1 Find $\displaystyle\int \frac{x}{\sqrt{1 + x^2}}\, dx$. You may wish to use the substitution $u = 1 + x^2$.

A $2\sqrt{1 + x^2} + c$　　　B $\sqrt{1 + x^2} + c$　　　C $u^{\frac{1}{2}} + c$　　　D $\frac{1}{2} \ln (1 + x^2) + c$

2 Find $\displaystyle\int \frac{6x^2}{1 + 4x^3}\, dx$.

Two of these answers are equivalent and both are correct. Look for both of them.

A $\frac{1}{2} \ln |1 + 4x^3| + c$　　　B $2 \ln |1 + 4x^3| + c$　　　C $\frac{2x^3}{x + x^4} + c$

D $2x^3 + \frac{3}{2} \ln |x| + c$　　　E $\frac{1}{2} \ln |2(1 + 4x^3)| + c$

3 The diagram shows a sketch of the curve $y = 10x(2x - 1)^3$.
Find the area of the shaded region using substitution $u = 2x - 1$.

A $\frac{1}{4}$　　　　　　　B 0.055

C $\frac{1}{8}$　　　　　　　D $-\frac{1}{8}$

4 The diagram shows a sketch of part of the curve $y = xe^{1-x^2}$.
Find the exact area of the shaded region which is between the curve, the x axis and the line $x = 1$.

A $\dfrac{1 - e}{2}$　　　　　　B $\dfrac{e - 1}{2}$

C $2(e - 1)$　　　　　　D $\frac{1}{2}e^{\frac{2}{3}}$

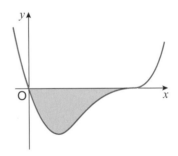

5 Find the exact value of $\displaystyle\int_{0}^{1} \frac{2e^x}{1 + e^x}\, dx$. You may wish to use the substitution $u - 1 + e^x$.

A $2 - 2 \ln 2$　　　B $\dfrac{2e}{1 + e} - 2$　　　C $\frac{1}{2} \ln \left(\dfrac{1 + e}{2} \right)$　　　D $2 \ln \left(\dfrac{1 + e}{2} \right)$

Exam-Style Question

i) Show that the substitution $u = 2x - 1$ can be used to transform the integral $\int \dfrac{x}{(2x-1)^2}\,dx$ into

$\dfrac{1}{4}\displaystyle\int \dfrac{u+1}{u^2}\,du.$

ii) Hence show the exact value of $\displaystyle\int_1^2 \dfrac{x}{(2x-1)^2}\,dx$ is $\dfrac{2+3\ln 3}{12}$.

Integrating trigonometric functions

A ABOUT THIS TOPIC

You have already seen how to differentiate $\sin x$ and $\cos x$. You can use the fact that integration is the reverse of differentiation to integrate these functions. You can then use integration by substitution to integrate functions involving $\sin x$ and $\cos x$.

R REMEMBER

- Differentiation of $\sin x$ and $\cos x$ from C3.
- Integration by substitution from C3.
- Trigonometric identities from C2.

K KEY FACTS

- $\int \cos ax \, dx = \dfrac{1}{a} \sin ax + c$

- $\int \sin ax \, dx = -\dfrac{1}{a} \cos ax + c$

You can use the fact that $\dfrac{d}{dx}(\sin x) = \cos x$ and the fact that integration

is the reverse of differentiation to say

$$\frac{d}{dx}(\sin x) = \cos x \quad \Rightarrow \quad \int \cos x \, dx = \sin x + c$$

And likewise,

$$\frac{d}{dx}(\cos x) = -\sin x \quad \Rightarrow \quad \int \sin x \, dx = -\cos x + c$$

You can integrate functions which are multiples of $\sin x$ and $\cos x$, such as $5 \sin x$ and $8 \cos x$, by inspection.

EXAMPLE 1

Find $\displaystyle\int_0^{\frac{\pi}{2}} (2 \cos x - \sin x) \, dx$.

SOLUTION

$$\int_0^{\frac{\pi}{2}} (2 \cos x - \sin x) \, dx = \Big[2 \sin x - (-\cos x) \Big]_0^{\frac{\pi}{2}}$$

Take care with your signs!

$$= \Big[2 \sin x + \cos x) \Big]_0^{\frac{\pi}{2}}$$

$$= \left[2 \sin \frac{\pi}{2} + \cos \frac{\pi}{2} \right] - [2 \sin 0 + \cos 0]$$

If you use your calculator then make sure it is in radians mode.

$$= [2 \times 1 + 0] - [2 \times 0 + 1]$$

$$= 2 - 1$$

$$= 1$$

Integration

You can use integration by substitution to integrate more complicated functions, as in the next examples.

EXAMPLE 2

Find $\int \cos 5x \, dx$.

SOLUTION

Let $u = 5x$ ◄──── *cos 5x is a function of a function. So use the substitution $u = 5x$.*

Convert dx to du

$$\frac{du}{dx} = 5 \implies \tfrac{1}{5} du = dx$$

Now substitute into the original integral

$$\int \cos 5x \, dx = \int \cos u \times \tfrac{1}{5} du$$ ◄──── *Replace 5x with u and dx with $\tfrac{1}{5} du$.*

$$= \int \tfrac{1}{5} \cos u \, du$$

$$= \tfrac{1}{5} \sin u + c$$

 Always remember to substitute back. You were asked to integrate a function of x so your final answer must also be a function of x.

To get the final answer replace u with $5x$

$$\int \cos 5x \, dx = \tfrac{1}{5} \sin 5x + c$$

This illustrates the general results that

$$\int \cos ax \, dx = \frac{1}{a} \sin ax + c$$

$$\int \sin ax \, dx = -\frac{1}{a} \cos ax + c$$

With practice you may find you can integrate a lot of trigonometric functions by inspection. But if you are in any doubt it is best to show all of your working.

EXAMPLE 3

The sketch shows the curve

$$y = \sin\left(3x + \frac{\pi}{4}\right).$$

Find the area of the shaded region.

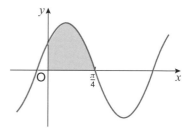

SOLUTION

You need to work out $\int_0^{\frac{\pi}{4}} \sin\left(3x + \frac{\pi}{4}\right) dx$.

Let $u = 3x + \dfrac{\pi}{4}$ ◄──── *Remember $\frac{\pi}{4}$ is just a number so when you differentiate it you get '0'.*

Convert dx to du

$$\frac{du}{dx} = 3 \implies \tfrac{1}{3} du = dx$$

You need to change the limits

$$x = \frac{\pi}{4} \implies u = 3 \times \frac{\pi}{4} + \frac{\pi}{4} = \pi$$

$$x = 0 \implies u = 3 \times 0 + \frac{\pi}{4} = \frac{\pi}{4}$$

Now substitute into the original integral

$$\int_0^{\frac{\pi}{4}} \sin\left(3x + \frac{\pi}{4}\right) dx = \int_{\frac{\pi}{4}}^{\pi} \sin u \times \frac{1}{3} \, du$$

> Replace $3x + \frac{\pi}{4}$ with u, dx with $\frac{1}{3} du$ and change the limits.

$$= \left[-\frac{1}{3} \cos u\right]_{\frac{\pi}{4}}^{\pi}$$

$$= \left(-\frac{1}{3} \times -1\right) - \left(-\frac{1}{3} \times \frac{1}{\sqrt{2}}\right)$$

$$= \frac{1}{3} + \frac{1}{3\sqrt{2}}$$

> This can be written as $\frac{\sqrt{2}}{3\sqrt{2}} + \frac{1}{3\sqrt{2}} = \frac{\sqrt{2} + 1}{3\sqrt{2}}$.

$$= \frac{\sqrt{2} + 1}{3\sqrt{2}}$$

> Rationalise the denominator by multiplying by $\frac{\sqrt{2}}{\sqrt{2}}$.

$$= \frac{2 + \sqrt{2}}{6}$$

EXAMPLE 4

Find the exact value of $\displaystyle\int_0^{\frac{\pi}{3}} \frac{\sin \theta}{1 + \cos \theta} \, d\theta$.

SOLUTION

Let $u = 1 + \cos \theta$

> $\frac{1}{1 + \cos \theta}$ is a 'function of a function' and the derivative of $1 + \cos \theta$ is $-\sin \theta$ so use the substitution $u = 1 + \cos \theta$.

Convert $d\theta$ to du

$$\frac{du}{d\theta} = -\sin \theta \implies -du = \sin \theta \, d\theta$$

> $-du$ means $-1 \, du$.

You need to change the limits

$$\theta = \frac{\pi}{3} \implies u = 1 + \cos \frac{\pi}{3} = 1 + \frac{1}{2} = \frac{3}{2}$$

$$\theta = 0 \implies u = 1 + \cos 0 = 1 + 1 = 2$$

Now substitute into the original integral

> Replace $1 + \cos \theta$ with u and $\sin \theta \, d\theta$ with $-1 \, du$ and change the limits.

$$\int_0^{\frac{\pi}{3}} \frac{\sin \theta}{1 + \cos \theta} \, d\theta = \int_2^{\frac{3}{2}} -\frac{1}{u} \, du$$

> ⚠ Take care that you get the limits the right way round.

$$= \left[-\ln u\right]_2^{\frac{3}{2}}$$

> Remember the rules of logs say: $n \ln a = \ln a^n$. So $-\ln \frac{3}{2} = \ln\left(\frac{3}{2}\right)^{-1} = \ln \frac{2}{3}$.

$$= \left(-\ln \frac{3}{2}\right) - (-\ln 2)$$

$$= \ln \frac{2}{3} + \ln 2$$

> Also: $\ln a + \ln b = \ln ab$.

$$= \ln \frac{4}{3}$$

> You were asked for the exact value so don't work this out.

EXAMPLE 5

Find $\int \sin x \, e^{1-\cos x} \, dx.$

$e^{1-\cos x}$ is a function of a function.

SOLUTION

Let $u = 1 - \cos x$

Convert dx to du

$$\frac{du}{dx} = \sin x \quad \Rightarrow \quad du = \sin x \, dx$$

Now substitute into the original integral

$$\int \sin x \, e^{1-\cos x} \, dx = \int e^{1-\cos x} \sin x \, dx$$

Replace $1 - \cos x$ with u and $\sin x \, dx$ with du.

Rewriting the integral like this makes it easier to see how to make the substitution.

$$= \int e^u \, du$$

$$= e^u + c$$

To get the final answer replace u with $1 - \cos x$

$$\int \sin x \, e^{1-\cos x} \, dx = e^{1-\cos x} + c$$

LINKS

Pure Mathematics	Integration (C4), Calculus (FP2), Differential Geometry (FP3), Differential Equations (DE), Numerical Methods.
Mechanics	Volumes of Revolution and Centres of Mass (M3), Variable Force and Mass (M4).
Statistics	Probability Density Functions (S3).

Test Yourself

1 Find $\int \left(\cos \frac{x}{2} - 3 \sin 3x\right) dx.$

A $-2 \sin \frac{x}{2} - \cos 3x + c$

B $-\frac{1}{2} \sin \frac{x}{2} - 9 \cos 3x + c$

C $2 \sin \frac{x}{2} + \cos 3x + c$

D $\frac{1}{2} \sin \frac{x}{2} + 9 \cos 3x + c$

2 Find the exact value of $\int_0^{\frac{\pi}{3}} \cos (2\theta - \pi) \, d\theta.$

A $-\frac{\sqrt{3}}{4}$

B $\frac{\sqrt{3}}{4}$

C $\frac{\sqrt{3}}{4} + \frac{\pi}{3}$

D $-\sqrt{3}$

3 Find $\int x^2 \cos (x^3) \, dx.$

A $3 \sin (x^3) + c$

B $-\frac{1}{3} \sin (x^3) + c$

C $\frac{1}{3} \sin u + c$

D $\frac{1}{3} \sin (x^3) + c$

4 The diagram shows a sketch of part of the curve $y = \dfrac{\cos x}{\sin x}$.

Calculate the exact area of the shaded region which is enclosed by the curve, the line $x = \dfrac{\pi}{3}$ and the x axis.

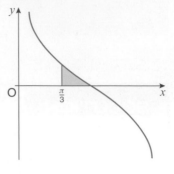

A   0.144

B $-\ln\left(\dfrac{\sqrt{3}}{2}\right)$

C $\ln\left(\dfrac{\sqrt{3}}{2}\right)$

D $\ln\dfrac{3}{2}$

5 Find $\displaystyle\int (\sin\theta\, e^{\cos\theta} - 1)\, d\theta$.

A $-e^{\cos\theta} - \theta + c$ B $-\cos\theta\, e^{\sin\theta} - \theta + c$ C $-e^{\cos\theta - 1} + c$ D $e^{\cos\theta} - \theta + c$

Exam-Style Question

a)   Find $\displaystyle\int \dfrac{\cos x}{e^{\sin x}}\, dx$.

b)   Show that $\displaystyle\int_0^{\frac{\pi}{6}} \dfrac{\sin 2x}{1 + \cos 2x}\, dx = \ln\left(\dfrac{2\sqrt{3}}{3}\right)$.

Integration by parts

ABOUT THIS TOPIC

You can now integrate a lot of functions but there is still one more useful technique to learn. Integration by parts enables you to integrate some products that can't be integrated by substitution.

R **REMEMBER**

- Differentiation of ln x, chain rule and product rule from C3.
- Integration of sin x, cos x and e^x from C3.
- Laws of indices from C1.

K **KEY FACTS**

- The formula for integrating by parts is:

$$\int u\,\frac{dv}{dx}\,dx = uv - \int v\,\frac{du}{dx}\,dx$$

- The formula for definite integration by parts is:

$$\int_a^b u\,\frac{dv}{dx}\,dx = \left[uv\right]_a^b - \int_a^b v\,\frac{du}{dx}\,dx$$

The formula for integration by parts comes from the product rule for differentiation and is:

$$\int u\,\frac{dv}{dx}\,dx = uv - \int v\,\frac{du}{dx}\,dx$$

Integration by parts can be used to integrate the product of two functions such as $x \sin x$ or $x^2 e^x$.

You need to decide which function to use as u and which function to use as $\frac{dv}{dx}$.

1 Choose u to be the function which becomes **simpler** when you **differentiate** it.

2 The other function will be $\frac{dv}{dx}$; check you can **integrate** it.

If this function can't be integrated then you need to change your choice.

Use the tables below and on page 68 to help you decide.

You can use integration by parts to integrate products of...	
a small polynomial in x like...	and a function of...
x $(x^2 - x)$ x^2	$\sin x$ $\cos x$ e^x
...choose as u	...choose as $\frac{dv}{dx}$

EXAMPLE 1

Find $\int 2x\mathrm{e}^{3x}\,\mathrm{d}x$.

SOLUTION

The derivative of $2x$ is 2 which is a simpler function.

The derivative of e^{3x} is $3\mathrm{e}^{3x}$ which is no simpler.

So choose u to be $2x$.

> Set out your work like this – then it is easier to use the formula.

> Differentiate u to find $\dfrac{\mathrm{d}u}{\mathrm{d}x}$.

Let $\qquad u = 2x \qquad \Rightarrow \qquad \dfrac{\mathrm{d}u}{\mathrm{d}x} = 2$

and $\qquad \dfrac{\mathrm{d}v}{\mathrm{d}x} = \mathrm{e}^{3x} \qquad \Rightarrow \qquad v = \dfrac{1}{3}\mathrm{e}^{3x}$

> Integrate $\dfrac{\mathrm{d}v}{\mathrm{d}x}$ to find v. Don't write '$+ c$' here otherwise you will end up with incorrect extra terms in your final answer.

Now substitute into the formula

$$\int u\,\frac{\mathrm{d}v}{\mathrm{d}x}\,\mathrm{d}x = uv - \int v\,\frac{\mathrm{d}u}{\mathrm{d}x}\,\mathrm{d}x$$

$$\int 2x\mathrm{e}^{3x}\,\mathrm{d}x = 2x \times \tfrac{1}{3}\mathrm{e}^{3x} - \int \tfrac{1}{3}\mathrm{e}^{3x} \times 2\,\mathrm{d}x$$

$$= \tfrac{2}{3}x\mathrm{e}^{3x} - \int \tfrac{2}{3}\mathrm{e}^{3x}\,\mathrm{d}x$$

$$= \tfrac{2}{3}x\mathrm{e}^{3x} - \tfrac{2}{3} \times \tfrac{1}{3}\mathrm{e}^{3x} + c$$

> Don't forget the '$+ c$'.

$$= \tfrac{2}{3}x\mathrm{e}^{3x} - \tfrac{2}{9}\mathrm{e}^{3x} + c$$

Sometimes you have to integrate by parts twice.

EXAMPLE 2

Find $\int x^2 \sin 2x\,\mathrm{d}x$.

SOLUTION

The derivative of x^2 is $2x$ which is a simpler function.

The derivative of $\sin 2x$ is $2\cos 2x$ which is no simpler.

So choose u to be x^2 rather than $\sin 2x$.

> Differentiate u to find $\dfrac{\mathrm{d}u}{\mathrm{d}x}$.

Let $\qquad u = x^2 \qquad \Rightarrow \qquad \dfrac{\mathrm{d}u}{\mathrm{d}x} = 2x$

And $\qquad \dfrac{\mathrm{d}v}{\mathrm{d}x} = \sin 2x \qquad \Rightarrow \qquad v = -\tfrac{1}{2}\cos 2x$

Now substitute into the formula

> Integrate $\dfrac{\mathrm{d}v}{\mathrm{d}x}$ to find v.

$$\int u\,\frac{\mathrm{d}v}{\mathrm{d}x}\,\mathrm{d}x = uv - \int v\,\frac{\mathrm{d}u}{\mathrm{d}x}\,\mathrm{d}x$$

> Take care with your signs! You will make fewer mistakes if you tidy up at this stage.

$$\int x^2 \sin 2x\,\mathrm{d}x = x^2 \times (-\tfrac{1}{2}\cos 2x) - \int (-\tfrac{1}{2}\cos 2x) \times 2x\,\mathrm{d}x$$

$$= -\tfrac{1}{2}x^2 \cos 2x + \int x \cos 2x\,\mathrm{d}x \qquad ①$$

> You can't integrate this directly so use parts again.

Using parts again on $\int x \cos 2x \, dx$

> This time choose u to be x.

Now let $\quad u = x \quad \Rightarrow \quad \dfrac{du}{dx} = 1$

and $\quad \dfrac{dv}{dx} = \cos 2x \quad \Rightarrow \quad v = \tfrac{1}{2} \sin 2x$

Now substitute into the formula

$$\int x \cos 2x \, dx = x \times \tfrac{1}{2} \sin 2x - \int \tfrac{1}{2} \sin 2x \, dx$$

$$= \tfrac{1}{2} x \sin 2x - \tfrac{1}{2} \times (-\tfrac{1}{2} \cos 2x) + c$$

$$= \tfrac{1}{2} x \sin 2x + \tfrac{1}{4} \cos 2x + c \qquad ②$$

> You haven't finished yet – remember you are trying to find $\int x^2 \sin 2x \, dx$.

Substitute ② into ①

$$\int x^2 \sin 2x \, dx = -\tfrac{1}{2} x^2 \cos 2x + \int x \cos 2x \, dx \qquad ①$$

$$= -\tfrac{1}{2} x^2 \cos 2x + \tfrac{1}{2} x \sin 2x + \tfrac{1}{4} \cos 2x + c$$

> Don't forget '$+ c$'.

> ⚠ Note: the order of the polynomial can tell you how many times you need to integrate by parts. In this case you had an x^2 so you had to use parts twice.

Sometimes it is not so obvious which function to choose for u and $\dfrac{dv}{dx}$.

EXAMPLE 3

Find $\int \ln x \, dx$.

SOLUTION

You can't integrate $\ln x$ by inspection but you can rewrite $\ln x$ as $1 \times \ln x$ so you have a product. Now that you have a product you can use integration by parts.

You should find $\int \ln x \, dx = \int 1 \times \ln x \, dx$.

You can't let $\dfrac{dv}{dx} = \ln x$ as you can't integrate it to find an expression for v.

So you have to choose u to be $\ln x$ and $\dfrac{dv}{dx}$ to be 1.

Let $\quad u = \ln x \Rightarrow \dfrac{du}{dx} = \dfrac{1}{x}$

and $\quad \dfrac{dv}{dx} = 1 \quad \Rightarrow \quad v = x$

> A common mistake is to think that the answer is $\dfrac{1}{x}$. But that's when you differentiate!

> ⚠ Notice $\ln x$ does become simpler when you differentiate it.

Now substitute into the formula

$$\int u \frac{dv}{dx} \, dx = uv - \int v \frac{du}{dx} \, dx$$

$$\int 1 \times \ln x \, dx = \ln x \times x - \int x \times \frac{1}{x} \, dx$$

> Simplify before you try to integrate.

$$= x \ln x - \int 1 \, dx$$

$$= x \ln x - x + c$$

This table will help you integrate functions which are a product of ln x and another function.

You can use integration by parts to integrate products of...		
A function of...	**and a small polynomial in x such as...**	
ln x	$x + 2$ x^2 1	
...choose as u	...choose as $\dfrac{\mathrm{d}v}{\mathrm{d}x}$	

To integrate ln x write it as $1 \times$ ln x and use parts.

You can also integrate definite integrals by parts using the formula:

$$\int_a^b u \, \frac{\mathrm{d}v}{\mathrm{d}x} \, \mathrm{d}x = \left[uv \right]_a^b - \int_a^b v \, \frac{\mathrm{d}u}{\mathrm{d}x} \, \mathrm{d}x$$

EXAMPLE 4

The diagram shows a sketch of part of the curve $y = -x \cos 2x$.

Find the area of the shaded region which lies between the curve, the axes and the line $x = \dfrac{\pi}{4}$.

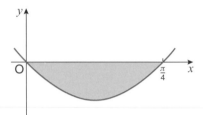

SOLUTION

You need to work out:

$$\int_0^{\frac{\pi}{4}} -x \cos 2x \, \mathrm{d}x$$

Let $\qquad u = -x \qquad \Rightarrow \qquad \dfrac{\mathrm{d}u}{\mathrm{d}x} = -1$

and $\qquad \dfrac{\mathrm{d}v}{\mathrm{d}x} = \cos 2x \qquad \Rightarrow \qquad v = \dfrac{1}{2} \sin 2x$

Now substitute into the formula

⚠ Take care with your signs! It is easier to tidy up as you go.

$$\int_a^b u \, \frac{\mathrm{d}v}{\mathrm{d}x} \, \mathrm{d}x = \left[uv \right]_a^b - \int_a^b v \, \frac{\mathrm{d}u}{\mathrm{d}x} \, \mathrm{d}x$$

$$\int_0^{\frac{\pi}{4}} -x \cos 2x \, \mathrm{d}x = \left[-x \times \frac{1}{2} \sin 2x \right]_0^{\frac{\pi}{4}} - \int_0^{\frac{\pi}{4}} \frac{1}{2} \sin 2x \times -1 \, \mathrm{d}x$$

$$= \left[-\frac{1}{2} x \sin 2x \right]_0^{\frac{\pi}{4}} + \int_0^{\frac{\pi}{4}} \frac{1}{2} \sin 2x \, \mathrm{d}x$$

If you use your calculator to work these out then make sure you are in radians mode.

$$= -\frac{1}{2} \left[x \sin 2x \right]_0^{\frac{\pi}{4}} + \left[\frac{1}{2} \times -\frac{1}{2} \cos 2x \right]_0^{\frac{\pi}{4}}$$

$$= -\frac{1}{2} \left[x \sin 2x \right]_0^{\frac{\pi}{4}} - \frac{1}{4} \left[\cos 2x \right]_0^{\frac{\pi}{4}}$$

$$= -\frac{1}{2}\left[\left\{\frac{\pi}{4} \times 1\right\} - \{0\}\right] - \frac{1}{4}\left[\{0\} - \{1\}\right]$$

$\sin\left(2 \times \frac{\pi}{4}\right) = 1.$

$\cos\left(2 \times \frac{\pi}{4}\right) = 0$ and $\cos 0 = 1.$

$$= -\frac{1}{2} \times \frac{\pi}{4} - \frac{1}{4} \times -1$$

$$= -\left(\frac{\pi}{8} - \frac{1}{4}\right)$$

$$= -\frac{(\pi - 2)}{8}$$

⚠ This integral is negative as the curve is below the x axis here.

So the area is $\dfrac{\pi - 2}{8}$.

You are looking for an area so you need to multiply the answer by -1 to make it positive.

LINKS

Pure Mathematics	Integration (C3, C4), Calculus (FP2), Differential Geometry (FP3), Differential Equations (DE), Numerical Methods.
Mechanics	Volumes of Revolution and Centres of Mass (M3), Variable Force and Mass (M4), Moments of Inertia.
Statistics	Probability Density Functions (S3), Variance.

Test Yourself

1 Find $\int (x + 1) \sin x \, dx$.

  A $-\left(\frac{1}{2} x^2 + x\right) \cos x + c$ B $(x + 1) \cos x + \sin x + c$

  C $-(x + 1) \cos x + \sin x + c$ D $(x + 1) \cos x - \sin x + c$

2 Find $\int x \ln 2x \, dx$.

  A $\frac{1}{2}x^2 \ln 2x - \frac{1}{4}x^2 + c$ B $\frac{1}{2}x^2 \ln 2x - \frac{1}{8}x^2 + c$

  C $\ln 2$ D $1 - \ln x + c$

3 Find $\int x^2 \cos x \, dx$.

  A $x^2 \sin x + 2x \cos x - 2 \sin x + c$ B $-x^2 \sin x + 2x \cos x - 2 \sin x + c$

  C $\frac{1}{3}x^3 \sin x + c$ D $-x^2 \sin x + 2x \cos x + 2 \sin x + c$

  E $x^2 \sin x - 2x \cos x + 2 \sin x + c$

4 Find $\int_0^1 x e^{2x} \, dx$.

  A $\dfrac{e^2}{4}$ B $2(2 - e^2)$ C $\frac{1}{2}x e^{2x} - \frac{1}{4}e^2 + \frac{1}{4}$ D $\frac{1}{4}(e^2 + 1)$

5 The diagram shows part of the curve $y = x \sin 2x$.
Find the exact area of the shaded region which lies between
the curve, the line $x = \dfrac{\pi}{3}$ and the x axis.

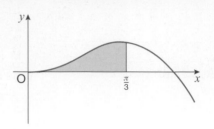

A $\dfrac{3\sqrt{3} - 2\pi}{24}$ B $\dfrac{\pi + 6\sqrt{3}}{2}$

C $\dfrac{2\pi + 3\sqrt{3}}{24}$ D $\dfrac{\pi^2}{72}$

Exam-Style Question

i)   Show that

$$\int x\mathrm{e}^{-x}\,\mathrm{d}x = -(x + 1)\mathrm{e}^{-x} + c.$$

ii) The diagram shows part of the curve $y = \dfrac{(1 - x^2)}{\mathrm{e}^x}$.
Find the x co-ordinates of the points where the curve cuts the x axis.

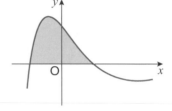

iii) Find the exact area of the shaded region which is between the
curve $y = \dfrac{(1 - x^2)}{\mathrm{e}^x}$ and the x axis.

Index

Formulae and results

Here are some formulae and results which you will need to recall or derive for the C3 examination. There is an underlying assumption that students already know all the results needed for GCSE Mathematics. You are also expected to recall or derive C1 and C2 results that are not given in the examination booklet. The following list is not exhaustive, and you should check with your teacher before your examination.

Exponentials

$y = e^x \Leftrightarrow x = \log_e y = \ln y$

$e^{\ln x} = x$

$\ln (e^x) = x$

Differentiation

Standard derivatives

$f(x)$	$f'(x)$
e^{kx}	ke^{kx}
$\ln x$	$\dfrac{1}{x}$
$\sin kx$	$k \cos kx$
$\cos kx$	$-k \sin kx$

Product rule

$y = uv \qquad \dfrac{dy}{dx} = u\dfrac{dv}{dx} + v\dfrac{du}{dx}$

Chain rule

y is a function of u and u is a function of x $\qquad \dfrac{dy}{dx} = \dfrac{dy}{du} \times \dfrac{du}{dx}$

Integration

Standard integrals

f(x)	$\int f(x)\, dx$ (+ a constant)
e^{kx}	$\dfrac{1}{k}e^{kx}$
$\dfrac{1}{x}$	$\ln|x|$
$\sin kx$	$-\dfrac{1}{k}\cos kx$
$\cos kx$	$\dfrac{1}{k}\sin kx$

Integration by substitution

$$y = f(u),\, u = g(x), \quad \int f'[g(x)]\, g'(x)\,dx = f[g(x)] + c$$